Ronald Reagan

Ronald Reagan

Michael Burgan

DK PUBLISHING

LONDON, NEW YORK, MUNICH,
MELBOURNE, AND DELHI

Editor : John Searcy
Editorial Director : Nancy Ellwood
Designer : Mark Johnson Davies
Art Editor : Jessica Park
Production Controller : Charlotte Oliver
Photo Research : Anne Burns Images

First American Edition, 2011

11 12 13 14 15 10 9 8 7 6 5 4 3 2 1

Published in the United States
by DK Publishing
375 Hudson Street
New York, New York 10014

DK books are available at special discounts
when purchased in bulk for sales
promotions, premiums, fund-raising,
or educational use. For details, contact:

DK Publishing Special Markets
375 Hudson Street
New York, New York 10014
SpecialSales@dk.com

A catalog record for this book is available
from the Library of Congress.

ISBN 978-0-7566-7074-0 (Paperback)
ISBN 978-0-7566-7075-7 (Hardcover)

Printed and bound in China
by South China Printing Co., Ltd.

Discover more at
www.dk.com

Contents

Prologue
A Historic Meeting
6–9

Chapter 1
Midwest Roots
10–19

Chapter 2
The Road to Hollywood
20–29

Chapter 3
The Communist Threat
30–37

Chapter 4
Staying in the Public Eye
38–45

Chapter 5
Launching a Political Career
46–53

Chapter 6
On the National Scene
54–61

Chapter 7
Run for the White House
62–71

Chapter 8
President Reagan
72–85

Chapter 9
Four More Years
86–97

Chapter 10
Iran, Contras,
and the President
98–105

Chapter 11
End of a Presidency
106–113

Chapter 12
Last Years
114–121

Timeline 122–123
For Further Study 124
Bibliography 125
Index 126

prologue

A Historic Meeting

In a cottage overlooking the Atlantic Ocean, the world's two most powerful leaders sat face to face. The house was said to be haunted, but President Ronald Reagan and Mikhail Gorbachev of the Soviet Union didn't seem concerned about ghosts. They had more important issues at hand.

On this chilly weekend in October 1986, the two leaders were in Reykjavik, Iceland, trying to settle differences between their countries. Since the end of World War II in 1945, the United States and the Soviet Union had been engaged in a power struggle known as the Cold War. Each sought to influence world events to its advantage while weakening its foe. To achieve this, the two countries had

During his presidency, Ronald Reagan held a number of important talks with Soviet leader Mikhail Gorbachev, including this one in Iceland.

built huge numbers of nuclear weapons—the most destructive weapons ever built. A single nuclear bomb could wipe out an entire city in an instant.

Reagan had long opposed the Soviet Union and its Communist government. But now he was ready to talk about reducing the number of nuclear arms each country built. Gorbachev suggested they each cut their supplies of certain large weapons in half. Later, the Soviet leader called for the elimination of all nuclear weapons within 10 years. Reagan distrusted the Russians, but he deeply feared the devastating effects of a nuclear war. He replied, "It would be fine with me if we eliminated all nuclear weapons."

However, there was a catch: Gorbachev wanted the United States to stop researching a missile defense system Reagan had proposed in 1983. The president wanted to prevent enemy missiles from reaching U.S. soil, either by destroying

Communism

Communism is a political system in which the government owns most property and provides many public services at no cost. Communist countries usually have just one political party, which controls the government. In general, Communist governments severely restrict their citizens' freedom, fearing any ideas or actions that might threaten their rule. In 1917, a revolution in Russia led to the world's first Communist nation, the Soviet Union.

them on their launching pads or by shooting them down in space. The plan was called the Strategic Defense Initiative, or SDI. Reagan's critics labeled the idea "Star Wars." Gorbachev worried that if the Americans had such a defense, they could safely launch a first strike on the Soviet Union, knowing the Soviets couldn't strike back. Reagan insisted SDI was purely for defense—and he would not consider ending the program.

Reagan was known for his sense of humor and positive approach to life. But now Gorbachev's position made him angry. Reagan realized that he and the Soviet leader were close to making a historic deal. Getting rid of so many nuclear weapons would be a major step toward world peace. Even so, Reagan had promised Americans he would develop SDI. He refused to break that promise. As his anger rose, Reagan stood up and said, "The meeting is over . . . we're leaving."

Outside, a cold rain fell. Reagan, usually eager to talk to the media, refused to provide a comment. His aides said that the president hadn't really expected to make any major agreements at Reykjavik. He merely hoped to pave the way for future talks.

By Monday, Reagan was in a better mood. He thought he and Gorbachev

The United States put missiles like these in Europe to counter Soviet missiles that targeted European cities.

had made progress, despite the meeting's abrupt ending. For the first time ever, the two Cold War foes had talked about getting rid of all of their nuclear weapons. Reagan insisted he still wanted to work toward that goal—but he wouldn't give up SDI

Reagan and Gorbachev lost their smiles by the time their Iceland meeting was over, with both men upset they could not reach an agreement.

to do it. Many Americans welcomed his position. They respected Reagan's desire for a strong military and his insistence on confronting the Soviet Union; it was one of the reasons they had elected him in 1980, and again in 1984. Yet Americans had also seen another side of their president—one that enabled him to talk to and work with his political foes. Reagan and Gorbachev had failed to reach an agreement in Iceland, but they had shown each other and the world that there was hope for the future.

Eventually, the arms cuts did come, and the Cold War ended after Reagan left office. He had played a key role in ending the Soviet threat to America's security. Today, Reagan is a hero to many Americans, especially those who share his views. But even those who dislike his politics recognize that he was one of the most important presidents in U.S. history.

chapter 1

Midwest Roots

During the 1840s, several million Irish people left their homeland, driven out by a deadly famine. Many of them settled in the United States. Some flocked into already-crowded cities; others headed for the open prairies of the American Midwest. Ronald Reagan's great-grandparents were among those Irish immigrants who headed west, looking for a better life for their family.

Ronald's father, Jack, was born in Fulton, Illinois, in 1883. Orphaned when he was only six years old, he spent most of his life near the banks of the Mississippi River. He played high-school baseball, then worked as a salesman in several Illinois towns. In 1904, Jack Reagan married Nelle Wilson in his hometown. The young couple

Ronald Reagan was born in an apartment above a bakery in Tampico, Illinois. The building later housed the First National Bank.

soon moved to Tampico, where Ronald Wilson Reagan was born on February 6, 1911.

As an adult, Ronald remembered his father as an ambitious man. Jack was always coming up with new ideas for making money. And he had a knack for telling stories and putting people at ease. His son called it "the gift of blarney and the charm of a leprechaun." Ronald would inherit some of his father's talent for telling a good story and making people like him.

The Reagans posed for this family portrait sometime around 1916. Ronald stands next to his mother Nelle.

But Jack Reagan also had a darker side, and battled alcoholism most of his adult life. When he was 11, Ronald (or "Dutch," as he was known) came home one evening and found his father passed out on the front steps. He dragged the much-larger man inside. Ronald later called this his first act of accepting responsibility. Even at that young age, he knew he had to take action to help his father and the family.

Although he seemed to get along well with others, Jack Reagan often had a grim view of people and life in general. His wife, though, was just the opposite. Ronald remembered his mother, Nelle, as someone who "always expected to find the best in people, and often did." She passed that optimistic attitude on to her son. However, the Reagans moved so often that Ronald had little time to form close friendships, a pattern that would continue later in life.

Nelle also influenced Ronald by raising him in her faith, the Disciples of Christ. At age 12, Ronald chose to become a member of that religion, while his older brother, Neil, remained in the Roman Catholic Church, like their father. Through his mother and the Disciples, Ronald came to believe that "God has a plan for everyone and that seemingly random twists of fate are all part of His plan."

A teenage Ronald Reagan poses in Dixon, Illinois, where his family rented five different homes during his boyhood.

Having a strong faith helped Nelle and Ronald survive some difficult years. Jack Reagan kept up the rambling ways of his youth, often moving his family from town to town. During one four-year stretch, Ronald attended four different schools. The family never had much money or owned its own home, and Ronald often ended up wearing his brother's hand-me-down clothes. Jack's alcoholism also sometimes cast a black cloud over the family. Coming home drunk, he would launch into loud, nasty arguments with his wife. Other times, he would mysteriously disappear for several days.

Still, Ronald later remembered his childhood as largely happy. He and his brother always had enough to eat and never felt poor. Ronald enjoyed roaming through hills or trying to catch wild animals, though without success. He spent many hours alone, drawing, studying wildlife, or reading adventure stories. He knew how to read at an early age, learning from his mother before he entered school.

The Disciples of Christ

Although it traced its roots to Scotland, Nelle and Ronald Reagan's religion was born in America. The Disciples of Christ believed people could use their intelligence to understand the Bible and find faith in God. They founded many colleges and libraries as they spread across the Midwest. The Disciples also stressed the need to love and serve others, as Jesus Christ did. Historically, the church's efforts included educating freed slaves and aiding the poor. Besides Ronald Reagan, two other U.S. presidents belonged to the Disciples of Christ: James A. Garfield and Lyndon B. Johnson.

Nelle also introduced Ronald to the stage. She had wanted to act, and she encouraged her son's efforts. They sometimes appeared together, each of them giving short speeches or reading stories. Ronald also acted in plays. After his first public performance, the audience applauded. He later wrote, "I liked that approval . . . when I walked off the stage that night, my life had changed."

The Reagans lived in this house in Dixon from 1920 to 1924. It is now listed in the National Register of Historic Places.

Despite all the family's travels, the Reagans managed to stay in Dixon, Illinois, for a long stretch of Ronald's childhood. He went to high school there, and he was a good student, showing a flair for writing. He also played football and swam. He tried playing baseball, but his bad vision made it hard, even after getting glasses—black-rimmed spectacles that he hated. Ronald also acted in school plays and served as president of his senior class.

During several summers, Ronald worked as a lifeguard at Lowell Park, along the Rock River. His father suggested he make a notch on a log for each swimmer he rescued, and over the years, Ronald recorded 77 notches. His heroics were sometimes featured on the front page of the local paper. A story from 1932 was titled, "'Dutch' Reagan Has Made Fine Mark as Guard—Dixon Youth Has Made 71 Rescues At Lowell Park Beach."

In 1928, Ronald entered Eureka College, in Eureka, Illinois. The school was run by the Disciples of Christ. Attending college was rare during the 1920s, something usually only children from wealthy families could afford. But Ronald was determined to go, and he convinced Eureka to give him a partial scholarship—money to help pay school costs. He worked to raise the rest of the money he needed. During the school year he washed dishes in the college's cafeteria, then returned to Dixon in the summers to work as a lifeguard.

> **STRIKE**
>
> In a strike, a group of people stops working as a form of protest.

Entering high school, Ronald had been a short, scrawny kid. Now, at 17, he was almost 6'1" (185 cm) tall and weighed a solid 175 pounds (79 kg). Although he was a good athlete, Ronald didn't make the football team as a freshman. He made his biggest mark that first year when the students at Eureka decided to go on strike.

As a lifeguard, Reagan often worked seven days a week, from early in the morning into the night.

The college was struggling to pay its bills, and the school president wanted to fire professors and make other changes to save money. Both students and professors opposed the plan, and for a time the students refused to go to classes. As the strike began, Ronald was picked to represent the freshmen; one student said it was because "he was the biggest mouth of the freshman class . . . a loud talker. Dutch was the guy you wanted to put up there." Ronald gave

Reagan's years as a lifeguard served him well at Eureka College, where he helped organize the school's first swim team and acted as a coach.

a speech outlining some of the students' concerns. Though he had spoken on stage before, this time was different. He was saying his own words, expressing ideas he believed in. Later he wrote: "For the first time in my life, I felt my words reach out and grab an audience, and it was exhilarating."

The strike lasted about two weeks and ended with the departure of the school president. Nevertheless, Eureka College would continue to endure tough times, as would the country itself. During Ronald's sophomore year, the United States faced a major financial crisis. In October 1929, the value of the country's major businesses began to plummet, and investors lost money. The country had already seen a rise in unemployment. Now, banks began to close as customers demanded their money. Fearful of more problems to come, people held onto their cash. Companies sold fewer goods, and more people were tossed out of work. Soon, the United States was immersed in the Great Depression, the worst economic

UNEMPLOYMENT

Unemployment is the state of not having a job. Nations try to keep unemployment rates as low as possible.

crisis it had ever experienced—and one that soon spread around the world.

As the Depression unfolded, Ronald sometimes had his own financial problems. He had to work more hours and borrow money from the school to pay his bills. Yet he still found time for a busy student life, as he played sports, acted in plays, and took part in student government. Finally, in 1932, he received his degree in economics and left Eureka. But the Depression had continued to worsen. After one more summer as a lifeguard, Ronald began his search for work.

He headed to Chicago, hoping to enter radio. At the time, radio was the only electronic source of news and entertainment

During the Great Depression, homeless people in many cities built small shacks in areas known as "Hoovervilles." The sites were named for President Herbert Hoover.

Reagan began his entertainment career behind a microphone at WOC radio in Davenport, Iowa.

available in the nation's homes. It was a growing industry, and Chicago was the radio capital of the Midwest. But Ronald had no experience as a broadcaster, and he came up empty in his job search. Determined to keep looking, he drove to the much smaller city of Davenport, Iowa. There, a local radio station called WOC agreed to try him as a sports announcer. Soon, "Dutch Reagan" was on the air, announcing college football games. The job ended in the fall, but in February 1933 the station offered him a full-time job. As luck would have it, the company that owned the station had a bigger one in Des Moines, Iowa's capital. Reagan was promoted to a position there in May.

By that time, American voters had made a huge political change. In the 1932 election, they rejected President Herbert Hoover, a Republican. To many Americans, Hoover had been too slow to realize the impact of the Great Depression and to soften the painful blows of the crisis. As a result, voters elected Democrat Franklin D. Roosevelt to replace him. Roosevelt had promised Americans a "New Deal" in which the government would start programs designed to end suffering and put people back to work.

Jack Reagan was one of the millions without a job during 1932. He and the rest of the Reagans were dedicated Democrats, with Ronald sometimes wearing a pin that supported "FDR." In the 1932 election, Ronald Reagan voted for the first time, and proudly picked Roosevelt. As Reagan later wrote, Roosevelt spoke in a "strong, gentle, confident voice" and "reassured us that we could lick any problem."

Roosevelt created new government agencies to help the poor and unemployed. One of these New Deal agencies soon hired Jack Reagan, as well as Ronald's brother, Neil. Then, thanks to his younger brother, Neil landed a radio job in Iowa. But it was Ronald who was about to become known across the Midwest.

Franklin D. Roosevelt

As president, Franklin D. Roosevelt often used the radio to address the nation, giving people hope during a dark time. Unlike Hoover, he was willing to expand the size of the government to try to end the Great Depression. His New Deal programs gave many people jobs, but the Depression ultimately didn't come to an end until World War II.

chapter **2**

The Road to Hollywood

In Des Moines, Ronald Reagan worked for radio station WHO, with a signal that reached millions of listeners. Many of them soon knew the voice of Dutch Reagan, who broadcast the baseball games of Chicago's two Major League Baseball teams, the Cubs and the White Sox. Reagan described every pitch, every hit, every out—without actually seeing any of the action.

Reagan covered many baseball events as an announcer for WHO, including the 1935 World Series— baseball's championship event.

To the listeners, it seemed as if Reagan were in the ballparks watching the games. In reality, he remained in the studios of WHO and received basic information from the stadiums by telegraph. Reagan then took those simple facts and described what was happening.

TELEGRAPH

The telegraph was an early form of long-distance communication, in which coded messages were sent along metal wires.

His words were so vivid, listeners couldn't tell he wasn't actually witnessing the action. Reagan called his performances "theater of the mind," and others noted the imagination and quick thinking it took to do the job well—especially on the day when the telegraph wire went dead in the middle of a Cubs game. Reagan described a believable, totally made-up scene to kill time until the signal was restored.

As a local radio star in Des Moines, Reagan made many public appearances to greet his fans. Here, he stops at a local high school.

Along with his baseball broadcasts, Reagan covered other sports for WHO. He also wrote about sports for a local newspaper, interviewed famous people who visited Des Moines, and spoke at public events in the region. He became something of an Iowa celebrity. Despite all this work, he still found time to enjoy himself. Reagan had always loved horses, and for the first time he learned to ride. A military-reserve program based in Des Moines kept horses and had an indoor riding ring. Reagan joined the program so he could ride as often as he wanted.

Across the country, millions were out of work, but Reagan's career was on the rise. Still, he hoped to do something beyond radio broadcasting—he wanted to become a movie actor. As it happened, baseball played a part in starting that new career.

Each year, the Chicago Cubs trained for the upcoming season on Catalina Island, off the California coast. The

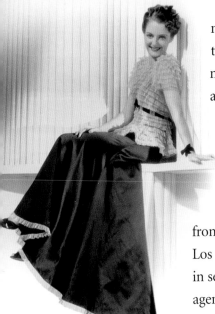

nearby city of Los Angeles was the center of the American movie industry. Starting in 1935, at Reagan's suggestion, WHO sent him to California to cover the Cubs' exhibition games. In 1937, Reagan took a break from his work to talk to Joy Hodges, a performer he knew from Iowa who now worked in Los Angeles. Hodges had appeared in several movies and knew an agent named Bill Meiklejohn. Reagan asked Hodges to help him meet Meiklejohn and begin an acting career. Her first suggestion was for him to take off his glasses, which he hated

Joy Hodges was a both a singer and a movie star, though she never won the fame her friend Ronald Reagan did.

so much. When Reagan went to meet the agent, he took her advice. "As a result," he later wrote, "I could hardly see him during one of the most important interviews of my life." But Meiklejohn saw that Reagan had good looks and a pleasant voice, important assets for a screen actor. The agent helped Reagan get a contract with Warner Brothers, one of Hollywood's major studios. He began his first movie that June.

At the time, almost all actors had contracts with a movie studio. They

> **AGENT**
>
> An agent is a person who helps an actor or artist find work.

only made movies for one company and had little choice about the roles they played. Reagan, like most new actors in Hollywood, started with "B" movies. Theaters often showed two movies together—called double features. The A movies had the biggest stars. The B movies featured lesser-known actors and the studios spent much less money to make them. But actors in B movies with talent or the right look could move up to A movies. Reagan quickly set out on that path.

Reagan was the perfect choice for his first role: He played a radio announcer in a movie called *Love Is on the Air*. Reagan had always been blessed with a sharp memory—some called it photographic. He took home the script for the movie and memorized it in just one night. The first day of shooting, he was nervous, but as soon as the camera went on, he relaxed. He thought, "You know, maybe I can make it here." When the movie was released, one of the local papers gave Reagan a good

The Hollywood Studios

The first American movies were made on the East Coast. By the 1910s, however, filmmakers began moving to California. The state offered warm weather, so they could film outdoors all year. It also had a variety of landscapes that could be used as the settings for movies. The major film companies soon settled in a part of Los Angeles called Hollywood—a name that came to represent the entire U.S. movie industry. Many studios are still based there.

Ronald Reagan and his wife Jane Wyman show off their first child, Maureen, in this photograph from 1941.

review. Soon, Warner Brothers gave him a new contract and a raise. The contract, however, was only for six months. He would still have to prove he could attract an audience and act in a variety of roles.

Over the next few years, Reagan played the lead role in many B movies. Often he played a newspaper reporter investigating a big crime or a government agent tracking down crooks. Directors found him easy to work with. He always came in on time and was always well prepared for his role. Each movie took about four weeks to shoot, with a typical day running about 12 hours. In his free time, Reagan continued to ride horses. He also spent time with friends who had followed him west from Iowa. Thanks to his hard work and confidence in himself, Reagan had built a life many people would have loved to live.

One of his new Hollywood pals was the actress Jane Wyman. They met while working together on a movie. At first she was just another of the friends Reagan spent time with outside of work. But their friendship soon turned into

a romance. They married in January 1940, and their first child, Maureen, was born the next year. Jane kept her stage name, because her movie career was advancing, just as her husband's was.

The same year he was married, Reagan appeared in one of his most famous movies: *Knute Rockne—All American.* The movie was based on the life story of Rockne, a football coach at the University of Notre Dame. Reagan practically begged to play the role of George Gipp, one of Rockne's former players. Reagan had long known about Gipp and thought he was perfect for the role. Finally, he won the part.

With his own background as a football player, Reagan was comfortable playing the part of George Gipp.

In the movie's key scene, Gipp is lying in a hospital bed, dying. He tells Rockne to someday tell one of his teams to "win just one for the Gipper." Later, when Notre Dame plays one of its biggest rivals, Rockne tells the story about the dying Gipp and his request. Notre Dame then goes on to win the game. In real life, Rockne probably made up the story about Gipp's words. Even Reagan doubted it was true. But the key point is that the story inspired the players to try

harder. And from then on, Reagan was always associated with the Gipper, and the idea of asking others to do their best.

Knute Rockne was an A movie. Another soon followed, a western called *Santa Fe Trail*. Reagan played George Custer, the officer famous for his defeat by the Lakota Indians at Little Bighorn. Reagan appeared with Errol Flynn, one of the biggest stars of the day. Although Reagan was usually not the leading actor in his movies, he was still a genuine star. He received fan mail from across the country

During the 1940s, carefully posed pictures of Ronald Reagan appeared in movie magazines, which told fans about the lives and work of their favorite stars.

and made enough money to move his parents to California and buy them a home.

Reagan's career received another boost after he starred in the 1942 movie *Kings Row*. Reagan considered it his best performance, and even before it was released, Warner Brothers offered him a new seven-year contract. Reagan had made an amazing journey. Ten years earlier, he was a small-town Midwestern radio broadcaster, lucky to make a few dollars per game. Now, he was one of the best-known actors in America, making a million dollars a year.

Those 10 years had also seen tremendous changes in the world around him. The Depression had dragged on, despite Roosevelt's New Deal. And overseas, Germany and Japan had become great military powers, eager to expand their control over neighboring nations. In 1937, following an earlier invasion, Japan launched an all-out war in China. Germany, led by Adolf Hitler, invaded Poland in 1939. Through the 1930s, most Americans wanted to stay out of the war. President Roosevelt, however, saw the threat Germany and Japan posed to the world's democracies. He tried to help Great Britain and France fight the Germans, even though Congress had not declared war.

German soldiers advance through France in 1940, part of Adolf Hitler's plan to control most of Europe.

As a boy, Reagan had watched soldiers go off to fight in World War I. Even at that young age, he knew some of the soldiers never returned from the battlefield, but were killed in combat. That war made him and many other Americans reluctant to engage in future foreign wars. However, he also realized that the nation could not isolate itself from world events. On December 7, 1941, Japan's surprise attack on Pearl Harbor, Hawaii, brought the United States into World War II. Soon, Reagan and millions of other Americans were all doing their part to help win the war.

Hollywood had been making war movies even before the attack on Pearl Harbor. In 1941, Reagan starred in *International Squadron.* He played an American pilot who volunteered to fly for the British. In real life, Reagan's bad eyesight kept him out of active military duty. But he served in the Army Air Corps and attained the rank of captain. Reagan belonged to a special Hollywood unit that made training films for the troops, along with other pictures meant to boost the spirits of soldiers and civilians alike. Reagan also spoke at events that raised money for the war effort.

During World War II, Reagan served in the Army Air Corps, which later became the U.S. Air Force.

As part of his job, Reagan reviewed films shot by soldiers in Europe and Asia. He saw some of the first footage taken at "death camps" run by the Germans. Hitler had sent Jews and other people he deemed inferior to these camps, where they were brutally murdered. Ultimately, six million European Jews were killed during the war, in a calamity known as the Holocaust. Watching the "ghastly images" of the camps shocked Reagan. He later called them "images on my mind that will be there forever."

The Atomic Bomb

Toward the end of World War II, British and American scientists developed a new weapon: the first nuclear (or atomic) bomb. This powerful weapon released the tremendous energy stored in tiny particles called atoms to produce a huge explosion and a deadly form of energy called radiation. In 1945, the Americans built two atomic bombs and dropped them on the Japanese cities of Hiroshima and Nagasaki. The two blasts killed several hundred thousand people and helped convince Japan to surrender.

Reagan had been lucky during the war. He didn't have to see the horrors of battle firsthand. He was able to spend most nights in his Los Angeles home. Still, like other Americans, he was glad when the fighting ended in August 1945. He was ready to go back to acting full-time. But as the "hot" war with Japan and Germany ended, the Cold War with the Soviet Union was about to begin.

chapter 3

The Communist Threat

The United States and the Soviet Union were allies during World War II. They and other countries fought together to defeat Germany and Japan. But after the war, the relationship between the Americans and the Soviets was sometimes tense. Each disliked the other's form of government and its economic system. Each wanted to prevent the other from influencing or controlling other nations. This simmering conflict became known as the Cold War.

Earlier, during the Great Depression, some Americans had thought Communism might be a way to end suffering and promote equality. They joined the Communist Party of the United States (CPUSA), which was heavily influenced by officials in Moscow, the

Soviet leader Joseph Stalin treated his citizens brutally, denying them freedoms, and arresting or killing anyone who opposed his rule.

A 1937 photograph shows members of the Screen Actors Guild in a union parade. SAG still protects the interests of actors in the United States.

Soviet capital. American Communists supported better wages and conditions for workers and equal rights for African-Americans. They turned a blind eye toward the harsh rule of the Communist Party in Russia, which denied citizens their freedoms, as well as the crimes of Soviet leader Joseph Stalin, who had killed several million of his own people to ensure his orders were followed.

In Hollywood, some people in the film industry joined the CPUSA. When Ronald Reagan began making films again after World War II, he saw their influence. Many workers in the industry belonged to unions. These groups try to protect the rights of workers and get them the best pay and benefits possible. In Hollywood, Communists sometimes played a major role in these unions.

Reagan and other film actors belonged to a union called the Screen Actors Guild (SAG). Although he didn't think

The Red Scare

Starting in the late 1940s, fears increased about the influence of Communists in the United States—a period known as the Red Scare. During this time, lawmakers accused many Americans of supporting Communism. The most famous anti-Communist was Senator Joe McCarthy, who falsely claimed that there were hundreds of Communists in the government and army. Today, such tactics are known as "McCarthyism."

workers should be required to join unions if they didn't want to, he saw how SAG helped all actors get the best benefits possible. By 1941, he had joined the union's board of directors, its top leadership. After the war, Reagan continued to serve on SAG's board of directors.

He also belonged to several groups that promoted New Deal goals. For the time being, Reagan remained a supporter of the Democratic Party and Franklin Roosevelt's policies—most of which were carried on after Roosevelt's death by President Harry S. Truman. As Reagan went to meetings, he saw Communists trying to influence or take over the groups. He disliked their methods as well as their message, which attacked the American form of government. His brother, Neil, also shaped his thoughts on Communists. Neil, now a Republican, argued that the Communists posed a threat to the country—a view that was

increasingly shared by Americans
of both political parties.

In March 1947, Reagan was
elected president of SAG. He would
hold that position for five years.

INFORMANT

An informant is someone who secretly gives information to the police or a government agency.

A few weeks after taking the job, Reagan was contacted by
the Federal Bureau of Investigation (FBI). This government
agency was closely watching the activities of the CPUSA and
the people who supported it. The FBI asked Reagan to help
by turning over any information he had about Hollywood
Communists. He gladly agreed, and the FBI gave him a code
name: He was informant T-10. Over the next several years, he
would meet with agents a few more times, revealing what he
knew about suspected Communists.

Reagan took a more public role in the hunt for Communists
later that year. In Congress, the House
of Representatives had a special

Ronald Reagan stands with
several other actors who spoke
out against Communists in
Hollywood. Some actors who
refused to cooperate with
Congress were not allowed
to make movies.

Ronald Reagan and Nancy Davis held their 1952 wedding at the home of fellow movie star William Holden (right).

committee investigating "un-American activities." It wanted to know more about the supposed Communist influence in Hollywood. Some actors, writers, and filmmakers refused to speak or did so only because they were threatened with legal action. Unlike these "hostile" witnesses, Reagan spoke freely about what he knew. He didn't say he knew any specific actor was a Communist. But he knew the party and groups close to it had "attempted to be a disruptive influence" in Hollywood, and that some members of SAG had "been suspected of more or less following the tactics that we associate with the Communist Party." Those tactics included spreading lies and concealing their ties to the Soviet Union.

Through the late 1940s, Reagan made films and remained active in the union. Meanwhile, Jane Wyman was also busy with her career, winning praise for her work. The couple had a second child, Michael, but the demands of raising a family and pursuing separate careers began to strain their marriage. They divorced in 1948, and the split surprised Reagan—

and hurt him. In his 1990 autobiography, Reagan mentions Wyman only briefly, in a few short sentences.

But Reagan was soon dating again, and in 1949 he met a young actress named Nancy Davis. Her stepfather was a wealthy Chicago doctor and her mother was a former actress. Davis began her film career appearing in several major movies. But after dating Reagan for a while, she took on a new role— Ronald Reagan's second wife. They were married on March 4, 1952, and soon had their first child, a girl named Patti.

That same year, Reagan made what many people considered his last good film, *The Winning Team.* He had also recently starred in a western, as

The Last Outpost was the third of three Ronald Reagan movies released in 1951. In another, *Bedtime for Bonzo*, Reagan appeared with a chimpanzee.

RONALD REAGAN

RHONDA FLEMING

THE

Color by TECHNICOLOR

LAST OUTPOST

A PARAMOUNT PICTURE

BRUCE BENNETT · BILL WILLIAMS · NOAH BEERY · PETER HANSON · LEWIS R. FOSTER · Written for the Screen by Geoffrey Homes, George Worthing Yates & Winston Miller · WILLIAM H. PINE & WILLIAM C. THOMAS he had dreamed of doing for so long. The film, *The Last Outpost,* did fairly well at the box office, but the studios didn't see Reagan as the best actor for lead roles in action movies. He was now over 40, and those parts usually went to younger men. Reagan's film career began to fade, but he soon switched over to a new form of entertainment. Television had been developed before World War II, but it didn't reach the general public until after the war. During the early 1950s, families increasingly bought

Reagan poses on the set of *General Electric Theater.* The show was the third-highest rated U.S. television program in 1956–1957.

TV sets for their homes, and TV networks needed plenty of shows to entertain them. Starting in September 1954, viewers saw Reagan host a show called *General Electric Theater,* named for the company that sponsored it, General Electric (GE). In addition to hosting, Reagan also sometimes acted in the episodes, which told a different story every week.

The television job paid well, at a time when Reagan was struggling for money. He made a large salary acting in movies, but the government collected a large portion of it in taxes. These taxes angered Reagan, who began to speak out against them. He thought actors paid too much in taxes. Over the years, he came to believe that all Americans paid too much, and that the government used the money to control more and more of their lives. These ideas became the core of his conservative beliefs.

In 1952, Reagan still belonged to the Democratic Party. But that year, he voted for Dwight D. Eisenhower, the Republican candidate for president. Reagan's views had changed during his years in Hollywood, as he came to see Communism as a growing threat to the nation. Like many other voters, he felt that Eisenhower would be a more effective opponent of Communism than President Truman. He also believed the federal government was becoming too big. Although he remained in television for many years, Reagan was already laying the foundation for a new career, as a politician.

Conservatives

Conservative describes a general attitude of wanting to preserve the best traditions from the past. In the United States, conservative people and parties usually favor a small federal government, promote religion, and support a strong military. On the opposite side of the spectrum are liberals, who tend to favor a larger government and to be more open to changing attitudes and values.

Political campaigns used a range of posters, pins, and other items to win support for their candidates.

LET'S CLEAN-UP *with* EISENHOWER *and* NIXON

chapter 4

Staying in the Public Eye

While still in Hollywood, Ronald Reagan found a way to earn extra money. He sometimes spoke to public groups, as he had done back in Iowa during his radio days. Reagan called it the "mashed potato circuit," since the meal served before he spoke usually included that dish. During these talks, Reagan expressed his conservative politics publicly for the first time.

Reagan liked to keep up with current events, and his experience as president of SAG had made him particularly interested in politics. As he worked for General Electric, he began to learn more about business as well. His new knowledge found its way into his speeches, which became more frequent as the 1950s went on.

General Electric made a wide range of products—from radios, televisions, and light bulbs to aircraft engines

A GE advertisement from 1955 promotes one of its products for the home, an electric stove and oven.

and plastics. It produced these goods in 135 factories spread across the country. Every year, GE sent Reagan on tour to visit the factories. At each one, he met with small groups of workers. His job was to boost their spirits and make them feel their distant GE bosses respected them and their work.

In 1955, Ronald Reagan visited a GE plant in his home state of Illinois. He estimated he met 250,000 GE workers during his tours for the company.

At first, Reagan mostly told jokes or stories about his days as a movie star. But over time, he focused on values that were important to him, such as limiting the size of government. GE saw how popular these talks were and had Reagan speak to groups of local citizens outside its factories, thinking Reagan's appeal could boost the company's sales.

As Reagan traveled across the country by train, he learned more about the problems of ordinary people. Over and

The Arms Race

As tension between the United States and Soviet Union mounted, each nation struggled to develop more and better weapons than its rival. Two key new technologies in this "arms race" were the hydrogen bomb, which was hundreds of times more powerful than the atomic bombs used in World War II, and the long-distance missile, which could be fired at targets thousands of miles away. By the 1960s, these devices had given the two countries the power to destroy each other almost instantly.

over, he heard concerns that "the ever-expanding federal government was encroaching on liberties we'd always taken for granted." At times, he would add some of the stories he heard from his audience to his speeches, as well as new information he'd read. Wherever he spoke, his main point was the same: Big business was good and the profits it made led to more wealth for everyone. Big government and rising taxes were bad. Reagan spread this message with a humor and certainty that convinced his audiences it was true. His talk was sometimes called simply "The Speech."

Although Reagan focused on domestic concerns, he didn't ignore world events. He still worried about the growing threat of the Soviet Union, which continued to build new weapons and sought to extend its

DOMESTIC

Domestic refers to issues within a particular country.

control over other nations. "Whether we admit it or not," he said, "we are in a war." Reagan believed the Soviet Union wanted to destroy capitalism, the economic system based on free markets that was used in the United States and other Western nations. The United States had to meet that threat overseas while trying to preserve freedom at home.

As he traveled and spoke, Reagan discussed serious issues. Yet he remained his usual smiling, upbeat self, brimming with confidence about his fellow citizens and their country. He had taken advantage of every opportunity he could and had built a good life. GE paid him well, he and Nancy had a second child, Ron, and the family owned a beautiful California ranch. When Reagan wasn't traveling, he spent time there riding horses, which was still one of his passions. But increasingly, politics was taking center stage.

In 1960, Reagan actively supported the Republican candidate for president, Vice President Richard Nixon. Reagan was still a Democrat, but his conservative ideas clashed with the party's goals. Reagan liked Nixon's strong anti-Communist views. The two men began a political

Ronald and Nancy Reagan's first ranch was located in the Malibu Mountains, not far from Hollywood.

One of Ronald Reagan's early political concerns was socialized medicine—health care run by the federal government.

relationship that lasted for decades. Sometimes they shared the same goals, and other times they didn't, but overall they respected each other.

Nixon lost his race for the presidency to John F. Kennedy. Two years later, in 1962, Nixon ran for governor of California. Once again, Reagan helped with Nixon's campaign, but Nixon lost again. Nevertheless, during the campaign, Reagan finally made the switch that had been coming for years: He left the Democratic Party and joined the Republicans.

That same year, General Electric canceled the show Reagan had hosted for so long, and he stopped making speeches for the company. But that didn't end Reagan's acting career. In 1964, he made one last movie and appeared on a few TV shows. In 1965, he was named the host of another TV show, a western called *Death Valley Days*. As for politics, cutting his ties to GE gave Reagan a greater chance to say exactly what he believed. Before, he had been careful to avoid any topics that might hurt GE's business. Now Reagan had complete freedom to make The Speech reflect all of his deeply held views.

These views were becoming even more anti-Communist, as Reagan spoke with different conservative groups. Some were upset that a revolution on the nearby island of Cuba had ushered in a Communist government there, one friendly to the Soviet Union. In October 1962, U.S. officials learned the Soviets had secretly sent nuclear missiles to Cuba. From there, the weapons could quickly wipe out most of the United States. People around the world feared that America and Russia would go to war over the missiles. The crisis ended peacefully, but Americans feared future conflict. Many conservatives now believed that President Kennedy was not doing enough to strengthen the U.S. military. And some thought the Republican Party was becoming too much like the Democratic Party, with many of its leaders seeming to accept the growing role of the federal government.

President John F. Kennedy was an important figure in the Cold War and convinced the Soviet Union to remove nuclear missiles from Cuba.

Reagan won great fame as a conservative when he campaigned for Barry Goldwater (left) during 1964.

In 1964, the Republicans chose a true conservative to run for the presidency: Senator Barry Goldwater of Arizona. Reagan had met him a few years before at Nancy's father's house. Reagan said, "I'd do anything I could to get him elected." That included giving speeches to help gain support for Goldwater. On October 27, Reagan gave a version of The Speech to the largest audience he had ever addressed.

A group of wealthy Goldwater supporters had bought time on a television network. They taped Reagan talking in front of a group of Republicans, then broadcast the speech to the nation. Reagan called his talk "A Time for Choosing." In Reagan's view, the country had a clear choice in the election, between more freedom under Goldwater or an ever-growing government under President Lyndon B. Johnson. He described the danger of high taxes and of letting a small group of leaders in Washington, D.C., "plan our lives for us." Reagan attacked the liberal belief that the government should play an active role in society to solve as many problems as possible. That kind of government, he believed, limited the freedom of all Americans.

In foreign affairs, he thought American liberals weren't tough enough when dealing with the Soviet Union. Instead, Reagan supported a strategy of "peace through strength." That meant building up the military and being willing to use it to stop the spread of Communism. According to Reagan, liberals accused conservatives of offering simple answers to difficult problems. "Well," he said, "perhaps there is a simple answer—not at an easy answer—but simple: If you and I have the courage to tell our elected officials that we want our national policy based on what we know in our hearts is morally right."

The broadcast of Reagan's speech didn't help Goldwater get elected. Too many Americans liked the policies of the Democrats or feared Goldwater would start a nuclear war with the Soviet Union. But the speech did make Ronald Reagan a rising star in the conservative political movement.

Barry Goldwater

Early in life, Barry Goldwater grew to dislike unions and government efforts to limit business. Even though he lost the 1964 presidential election, he is considered the "father" of the modern conservative movement in the United States. After that election, the Republican Party became more intensely conservative—a trend that has continued to the present day.

chapter 5

Launching a Political Career

Conservative leaders in California saw the impact of Reagan's speech for Goldwater. After the broadcast, people from across the country donated millions of dollars to Goldwater's campaign. Some California conservatives asked Reagan several times to run for governor in their state. He was interested, but didn't commit himself to running.

Reagan wrote years later that he had never thought about running for political office: "I had a good job and a good life, and, at 54, the last thing I wanted to do was

Where's the Rest of Me?

The Autobiography of
RONALD REAGAN
with Richard G. Hubler

to start a new career." In 1964, he wrote an autobiography called *Where's the Rest of Me?*, published the following year. In that book, he mentioned that even before the Goldwater campaign, some people had asked him to enter politics. He said he would rather talk

The title of Reagan's 1965 autobiography came from a line he spoke in one of his best-known movies, *Kings Row*.

Before his run for governor, Reagan visited such spots as Big Sur, a 90-mile (145 km) stretch of California coastline.

about political issues than work in the government. But at least one historian thinks the book was actually Reagan's first step in a plan to run for office.

California conservatives kept pressuring Reagan. Finally, he agreed to travel across California and see how many people might support him if he ran. The Republicans in the state were divided between strict conservatives and more moderate members. And Democrats were in the majority in California. Reagan, with no political experience, would face a tough campaign if he ran.

California is a huge state, some 800 miles (1,287 km) long. Reagan spent six months driving to its distant corners, from the mountains to the deserts to the Pacific coast. He spoke to local groups and met one-on-one with voters. Finally, at the end of the year, he made his decision: He was in the race.

His conservative backers called in experts to help Reagan learn how to run a campaign. He knew little about California politics, but, according to one early supporter, "he was sure good on his feet." The years he had spent on radio, in films, and making speeches put Reagan at ease in front of crowds. Like his father decades before, he had charm that attracted people to him. And Reagan stressed that his lack of political experience was actually a good thing. He said, "I am an ordinary citizen with the deep-seated belief that much of what troubles us has been brought on by politicians."

Even after professional coaching, Reagan sometimes made factual errors when he spoke, but he used humor to win people over. And he addressed issues that concerned a growing number of Californians. For example, students at one state college were protesting the Vietnam War, which had begun

Like any good politician, Reagan enjoyed meeting with voters, as he does here shortly after announcing his run for governor.

several years before. Reagan said the state should crack down on any troublemakers and restore order. Reagan also talked about violence among some African-Americans. In 1965, riots had broken out in Watts, a black community in Los Angeles. Some young black leaders promoted the use of violence to achieve racial equality. Reagan promised to end the violence as well as the government policies that added to racial conflict.

Reagan won the nomination to be the Republican Party's candidate for governor. Then, he crisscrossed the state again,

The Vietnam War

The Vietnam War was one part of the Cold War that got "hot," with fighting that lasted for more than 20 years. The United States became heavily involved in the 1960s, supporting South Vietnam while the Soviet Union supported North Vietnam, which was trying to unite the country under a Communist government. As the war dragged on, it became increasingly unpopular with American citizens. The last U.S. troops finally left in 1975, and the country was soon under Communist control.

seeking votes in the fall election. Despite a lifelong fear of flying, he finally agreed to travel by airplane. He realized he had to quickly cover a lot of ground and speak to as many people as he could. Reagan had never campaigned before, but he was surrounded by professionals who informed him on key issues and kept him focused on winning votes.

California's sitting governor, Pat Brown, didn't take his new opponent seriously. All the governor saw was "an aging actor" with extreme views. But Reagan had distanced himself from some of the extreme California conservatives, while still pushing his usual message: Cut taxes. Reduce the role of government. Preserve traditional American values.

Ronald and Nancy Reagan celebrate his election as governor. Reagan won the race by more than 1.3 million votes.

On November 8, 1966, the voters of California elected Ronald Reagan as the state's 33rd governor. Reagan now had just two months to choose the people who would help him run the state. He also needed to prepare a budget before he even took office. Since he'd been focusing entirely on the campaign, Reagan hadn't realized this. His strength was in describing the big picture of what government should or shouldn't do. He wasn't as interested in the small points of governing from one day to the next.

Reagan was sworn in as governor just after midnight on January 3, 1967. He wanted to show people his desire to get right to work and make changes.

ADMINISTRATION

A leader's administration refers to the various aides and department heads who work with him or her to run the government.

But he faced several big problems. Many members of his administration lacked experience in government. At the time, California was confronting a huge economic crisis. The state needed money to provide all the services the people wanted. But Pat Brown had refused to increase taxes or cut spending. Now Reagan would have to make some difficult decisions. To make matters worse, he had to convince the state's lawmakers to go along with his plans. The leaders of the legislature (the branch of government that makes laws) were Democrats, and many of them were skeptical about Reagan's ideas.

The biggest problem Reagan faced when he took office was the budget. For a year, the state had been spending more money that it took in. To help fix this, he proposed that all state agencies cut their spending by 10 percent. Many saw these cuts as unfair, since they treated well-run agencies the same as ones that had been wasting money. (In the end, he withdrew most of the cuts.) At the same time, Reagan persuaded the legislature to pass a massive tax increase—larger than any state in history had ever passed. No one liked the

As governor, Reagan had to sign bills passed by the General Assembly before they could become laws.

Choosing a Presidential Candidate

Early in the U.S. presidential election process, candidates within the major parties compete for votes state by state in special elections called primaries. By winning primaries, the candidates obtain the support of people called delegates. At each party's national convention, the delegates vote to determine who will be that party's official candidate in the main election in November.

tax hike, but across the state, few people blamed Reagan. Most realized that he had inherited problems that started when Brown was governor. And in the years that followed, the government was able to give back some of the new tax money it had taken in.

Addressing the budget crisis, Reagan learned how to deal with the lawmakers. If they voted for something he wanted, he would do something for them. He also chose new advisors with more experience, helping the government run more smoothly. Reagan learned on the job, and he remained mostly popular with the voters.

Fixing California's economic woes filled Reagan's first year in office. Then, in 1968, he considered a new endeavor: running for president. After he finished a speech, Reagan often heard supporters say he should seek the nation's highest office. Reagan told them he wasn't interested. But as early as the fall of 1967, national political reporters wrote about a quiet plan among Reagan's advisors to have him seek the nomination.

As Reagan later explained, some Republican Party leaders in California pressed him to run for president. Across the country, the party was divided between moderates and conservatives. If Reagan ran for the nomination just in the California primary, he might be able to help unite the party. He would most likely win the votes of all of California's many delegates to the Republican convention. Those votes would give Reagan some influence in working with the party's two sides. Reagan soon agreed to this plan.

For a time, Reagan didn't actively campaign. But wealthy supporters put up money so a Reagan aide could begin to recruit support for him. Then, in the summer of 1968, after making speeches across the country, Reagan officially declared himself a national candidate for president. The announcement came at the Republican convention, where the party would choose its candidate. By then, however, most Republicans supported Richard Nixon. Seeing this, Reagan spoke to the convention and offered his support to Nixon. In private, Reagan was relieved. He told an aide, "I just didn't think I was ready for it." Reagan soon went back to his duties as governor. But across the country, conservatives still saw him as a rising political force.

Nancy Reagan enjoys the support shown for her husband during the 1968 Republican convention.

chapter **6**

On the National Scene

Reagan's first run for the presidency was short-lived, and he soon returned his attention to California. His efforts to end protests at the state's universities and colleges continued to be popular with voters, but less so with students and teachers. In some cases, there were violent clashes between demonstrators and police. Eventually, calm returned to the campuses, but Reagan's major goals of reforming government and reducing its size were still unfulfilled at the end of his first term. By the end of 1969, he later wrote, "I realized I was going to need more time

This 1969 protest at People's Park in Berkeley, California, was one of several that Reagan dealt with as governor.

than I had left in my first term to accomplish my goals as governor, and I had enough experience—and enjoyment—at it to know I didn't want to stop."

In 1971, Reagan met with President Richard Nixon to discuss a range of topics, including welfare reform.

Reagan won his race for reelection in 1970 and soon turned to what he saw as a growing problem: the state's welfare system. This government program provided money to the poor, and was expanding rapidly due to a change in the law. Many local officials feared they wouldn't be able to keep paying for it. Reagan blamed "welfare cheats," who he claimed were taking money illegally. Democrats said that Reagan was focusing too much on welfare fraud. They claimed welfare costs were increasing mostly because there weren't enough jobs available for poor people.

For several months in 1971, Reagan and his aides battled Democrats over his proposed changes to California's welfare system. Reagan was willing to raise the amount of money people received, but he wanted to make it harder for them to collect it. The Democrats were ready to make some changes, but not as many as Reagan wanted. Bob Moretti, the leader of the Democratic lawmakers, thought Reagan lived in "a world of unreality." But he also thought he and Reagan

The Great Society

As a young man, Ronald Reagan supported the New Deal. But he strongly opposed the new "Great Society" programs started by President Lyndon B. Johnson in the 1960s. Johnson and other Democrats were trying to wage a "war on poverty" by extending medical aid and other help to the poor. Critics, such as Reagan, said the Great Society did not do much to end poverty—it simply raised taxes and increased the size of the government.

should try to work together to pass welfare reform.

When the two sides met, shouts often filled the room. When Reagan showed his anger, Moretti was convinced he was using some of his old acting talents, pretending to be madder than he was simply to shake the Democrats. But Reagan was not faking when it came to his beliefs. He accepted the idea of individual responsibility, the idea he had first demonstrated many years before when helping his drunken father. People had to act on their own, take care of themselves. Yet, as a politician, he knew that at times he had to compromise to get anything meaningful done.

Through a series of long talks, Reagan and Moretti achieved welfare reform that gave each side some of what it wanted. The new law let people collect more money, but gave the government more authotity to crack down on fraud.

The number of people on welfare soon began dropping. The California system soon became a model for other states, and Reagan won praise for his efforts to take people off of welfare and try to get them back to work.

Reagan also enjoyed other successes during his second term, as the state continued to give back tax money collected after the earlier increase. He also supported a law to limit local property taxes, though the result was an increase in other taxes. In 1973, Reagan began another effort at tax reform. He supported Proposition 1, which called for strict limits to be set on state spending, based on how much money residents made as a whole. The controversial proposition would also make it harder for state lawmakers to pass new taxes. The details of the proposal were complex, and Reagan didn't help his cause when he once joked that even he didn't understand it. In the 1973 election, Californians rejected Proposition 1.

Some political observers thought the proposed tax changes were not just about California. They believed that Reagan was already considering running for president in 1976, and that he wanted

An opponent of Proposition 1 talks to Nancy Reagan. In the end, 54 percent of voters rejected the taxing-and-spending proposal.

On August 9, 1974, Richard Nixon left the White House after resigning the presidency.

to show conservatives across the country how serious he was about cutting taxes. Throughout his last two years as governor, Reagan took several steps that suggested he was considering another run for the White House. He traveled across the country making speeches, and during 1974 his aides met frequently to discuss how much support he was winning. But events that year soon changed the outlook for 1976.

On August 8, 1974, Richard Nixon resigned as president, seeking to avoid impeachment because of the Watergate scandal. His vice president, Gerald Ford, then took over the presidency. Most Republicans assumed that Ford would seek a full four-year term in 1976. Reagan would have a much harder race against Ford, an incumbent, than in a wide-open field of many

> **INCUMBENT**
>
> An incumbent is the person who currently holds an elected position.

Republican candidates. Nevertheless, Reagan made plans to run for president.

After leaving the governor's office and before he officially began his campaign, Reagan took a familiar position: sitting behind a radio microphone. O'Connor Creative Services of California hired him to give a short, daily radio address, broadcast on several hundred stations across the country. He also began writing a weekly newspaper column that reached a national audience. As in his GE days, he did all the writing himself, using a pen or pencil and yellow lined paper. And, as in those years of traveling and speaking across the country, Reagan laid out his conservative views.

As 1976 began, Reagan's campaign to win the Republican presidential nomination began in earnest. Although most conservatives liked him, many felt they should be

Watergate

In June 1972, men connected to Nixon were arrested for breaking into the Democratic Party headquarters, located in the Watergate office building. Nixon denied knowing about the break-in, then tried to hide his connection to the crime. Slowly the truth emerged, and by August 1974, Congress was ready to impeach Nixon—which would have forced him to stand trial, and possibly be removed from office. Rather than face this process, he decided to resign.

loyal to President Ford. Reagan seemed to be breaking what he and others called their party's Eleventh Commandment:

Reagan supporters cheer his victory in the 1976 North Carolina primary. Reagan won the delegates of 11 states.

Republicans should not say bad things about other Republicans. Reagan had once vowed to obey the commandment, but he had already attacked Ford's handling of relations with the Soviet Union. The criticisms continued as the campaign went on.

Reagan focused his time and money on three early primaries, hoping that wins in those states would attract more support later on. However, some of his proposals didn't sit well with many Americans. In one plan, he called for cutting federal taxes and transferring responsibility for some federal programs to the states. But states that had low taxes would have had to raise them to pay for the services. One of the states Reagan was focusing on in the primaries was New Hampshire, which had no income tax at all. Ford claimed that, under Reagan's plan, the state would be forced to adopt one—an idea that most of the state's voters were against.

Ultimately, Reagan lost New Hampshire, along with the other early primaries he targeted, but he bounced back with victories in some key states, including Texas and California. In August, he went to the national convention with a good chance to win the nomination. But when the votes were cast, Ford won a slim victory. He would be the Republican candidate. In the general election, he would face Democrat Jimmy Carter, a former governor of Georgia.

In a radio address after his campaign, Reagan stressed the good that had come out of his loss. He was glad for the chance to travel around the country and meet so many Americans. He remained convinced "of the greatness of our people and their capacity to determine their own destiny." And he still believed most Americans wanted smaller government.

Reagan and Gerald Ford meet at the 1976 Republican convention, where Reagan lost by a slim margin.

For Reagan, the 1976 loss had another important impact: It cemented his reputation as the country's leading political conservative. Few doubted he would be back when the next presidential election came.

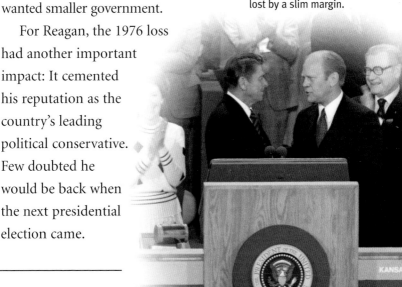

chapter **7**

Run for the White House

In the 1976 presidential election, Gerald Ford lost to Jimmy Carter. Some political experts saw the Democrat's victory as the voters' reactions to the previous eight years. Nixon had dragged out the Vietnam War, after promising in 1968 to end it. Then he lied about Watergate. Ford didn't help his own cause when he pardoned Nixon, meaning the former president could never be tried for any crimes he might have committed while in office.

Before becoming president, Jimmy Carter had served in the U.S. Navy and run his family's peanut farm.

Even before Carter's presidency began, Reagan was back delivering

his radio addresses and writing his columns. Over the next four years, he often criticized Carter's policies. Reagan opposed the president's efforts to lower taxes for some people while raising taxes for wealthier Americans. He said the president was trying to get "the most feathers possible from the fewest geese in order to minimize the quacking." To Reagan, the key was cutting government spending, not raising taxes on anyone. And if the rich received tax cuts, he reasoned, they would probably invest their money in businesses that would create new and better jobs. These new workers would then pay taxes, helping to make up for the cuts.

After his 1976 loss to Gerald Ford, Reagan once again took to the airwaves to broadcast his views.

In foreign policy, Reagan thought Carter was not firm enough when dealing with the Russians. Reagan wanted a larger military with the best weapons possible. He opposed détente, a policy favored by Richard Nixon, under which the United States and Soviet Union negotiated to keep their nuclear stockpiles evenly balanced. Reagan worried that America "could find itself isolated in a hostile world with a succession of bitter choices between war and surrender." Either option would be horrible for the country.

Several times during the 1970s, events in the Middle East created shortages of gasoline, leading to long lines at the pump.

By the fall of 1979, Carter faced many challenges.

Politically, he was losing support from more liberal Democrats, who thought he had not done enough to help average Americans. Carter had often struggled to win support for his policies from Congress, and sometimes lacked the skills to make deals or seek compromise. The economy had weakened, with inflation and unemployment both beginning to rise. Oil prices had also risen sharply, as a revolution broke out in Iran, a major supplier of oil. In July 1979, Carter spoke to the nation about the range of national problems and the growing dark mood of the people. He talked about a "crisis of confidence," but the solutions he offered didn't seem to please most Americans.

The worst blow for the Carter presidency came that November. On the fourth of that month, students in Iran kidnapped

INFLATION

Inflation is an economic condition marked by rapidly rising prices and wages.

dozens of Americans, with the permission of the country's new ruler, Ayatollah Ruhollah Khomeini. A few were released, but 52 Americans would remain captive. In April 1980, Carter ordered a secret rescue mission, which failed. Once again, many Americans saw their president as someone who couldn't solve the country's biggest problems.

By the time of the botched rescue, the 1980 presidential campaign was in full swing. Reagan had announced his candidacy a few months before, joining nine other Republicans seeking the party's nomination. When he first entered the race, Reagan addressed the mood he sensed in Washington. Leaders there were "reduced to bickering with each other and [are] no longer possessed of the will to cope with our problems. Much of this talk has come from leaders who claim that our problems are too difficult to handle. We are supposed to

Trouble in Iran

Starting in the 1950s, the United States supported the reign of Shah Mohammed Reza Pahlavi in Iran. Although the shah ruled as a dictator, the U.S. accepted his harsh regime, mainly because he opposed Communism. In 1979, a Muslim religious leader, Ayatollah Khomeini, led a revolution that forced the shah from power. When President Carter let the shah come to the United States for medical treatment, the Iranians took their American hostages.

meekly accept their failures as the most which humanly can be done. They tell us we must learn to live with less, and teach our children that their lives will be less full and prosperous than ours have been; that the America of the coming years will be a place where—because of our past excesses—it will be impossible to dream and make those dreams come true. I don't believe that. And, I don't believe you do either."

With that speech, Reagan

The Religious Right

Fundamentalists are members of a religion who strictly follow their faith's basic teachings—the fundamentals. Starting with the Reagan campaign, fundamentalist Christians have played an important role in U.S. politics. They and others with strict religious views have been called the "religious right." (In general, "the right" refers to conservatives, while "the left" refers to liberals.) The religious right tends to oppose abortion and increased legal rights for homosexuals, and to support prayer in schools and the influence of Christianity in society.

set the tone for his campaign. He would attack what he saw as Carter's flaws. And he would offer Americans hope for a better future—the same message he had been giving for almost 25 years.

Although Reagan and Bush were rivals in the primary, they later joined forces.

But before he could take on Carter, Reagan had to confront the other Republicans seeking the nomination. Reagan was clearly the favorite of conservatives. By now, their ranks had increased, as fundamentalist Christians started taking a more active role in politics. They believed they were part of a "moral majority" whose views had been ignored in Washington. Conservatives were less drawn to Reagan's major challenger, George Bush. He had held several different important positions in Washington, but he was considered a more moderate Republican.

In addition to offering hope, Reagan told voters he had a very specific plan for the economy. He would cut taxes, reduce the deficit, and increase military spending. Bush didn't think it was possible to bring in more revenue while lowering taxes— he called the idea "voodoo economics." He said it would take some kind of magical spell to do everything Reagan proposed.

In January 1980, Bush won the first nominating event, a caucus

The Reagans campaign in South Carolina during the 1980 presidential election. Reagan was popular there and across most of the South.

The only debate between Jimmy Carter and Ronald Reagan was held in Ohio, a state Reagan won during the election that followed.

in Iowa. Reagan came back with a solid win in New Hampshire, followed by more victories. As the other candidates dropped out, only Bush remained, but he was able to win just four states to Reagan's 29. By May, Reagan was the clear winner, which the Republicans confirmed at their national convention in July. For a time, Reagan considered naming Gerald Ford as his vice presidential running mate. In the end, he chose Bush. Reagan later wrote, "I had always liked him personally and had great respect for his abilities." Bush also balanced Reagan's political views, since he was not as conservative.

The two Republicans traveled across the country, telling Americans how Carter had failed them. Inflation had continued to soar, reaching its highest level in more than two decades. At the same time, unemployment was also high. In foreign affairs, Reagan claimed that Carter had failed to restrain Soviet actions around the world. By this time, the Russians had invaded Afghanistan, seeking to support a Communist government there. Also, the 52 hostages were still being held in Iran. But despite all these problems, Reagan saw a bigger issue, fueled by these concerns: "America had lost faith in itself." His goal was to help Americans "recapture our dreams, our pride in ourselves and our country."

With the election just a week away, Reagan and Carter met in a debate. Carter, as usual, was well informed, but he seemed less comfortable in the face-off than Reagan, who accused the president of distorting his position on various issues. At one point, he turned to Carter and said, "There you go again." Later, Reagan asked the viewers a question: "Are you better off than you were four years ago?" That question has been repeated often since 1980, whenever political candidates challenge a struggling incumbent.

For Reagan, the question helped convince voters he should be the next president. They weren't better off, they didn't want four more years of Carter, and they thought Reagan could turn the country around.

A newspaper predicts what actually happened—Reagan's easy victory over Jimmy Carter.

Reagan was back in California on Election Day, November 4. Voters there were still going to the polls when he received a call. President Carter had seen the early results from the

Eastern states, where polls were already closed. He knew he couldn't win.

He wanted to congratulate Reagan, who had just been elected the 40th president of the United States. At the age of 69, Reagan would be the oldest incoming president in history. But he was healthy and energetic, ready for the responsibility he now faced.

Reagan's term as president wouldn't begin until January 20, 1981. During the next few months, he chose his cabinet, the men and women who would lead federal departments and offer him advice. He also prepared a speech for his inauguration ceremony to set the tone for the next four years.

Ronald Reagan delivers his Inaugural Address, with the monument honoring George Washington, the first U.S. president, in the distance.

Early on the morning of January 20, Reagan received good news. Carter called to say that after long talks, the Iranians had agreed to release their American hostages. Reagan thanked Carter and asked him to fly to Germany to greet the hostages after they were released. However, no one knew for sure when this would happen, and both men agreed not to say anything until they knew for sure that the hostages were out of Iran. So, in his inaugural speech, Reagan didn't mention the hostages. Instead, he commented on the country's economic problems, and the hard work required to fix them. He promised to reduce the size of the government. He called for peace, but said the United States would always be ready to defend itself and help people in other nations win their freedom.

Near the end of the speech, Reagan told a story about a young soldier who gave his life for the United States during World War I. According to Reagan, Americans didn't have to match that soldier's sacrifice. But the current problems, he said, "require . . . our best effort, and our willingness to believe in ourselves and to believe in our capacity to perform great deeds; to believe that together, with God's help, we can and will resolve the problems which now confront us. And, after all, why shouldn't we believe that? We are Americans." During the next four years, Americans would see Reagan demonstrate his faith in them and himself again and again.

Inauguration Day included a parade, shown here, and 10 parties celebrating the Reagan presidency.

chapter **8**

President Reagan

Ronald Reagan had faced many challenges as governor of California. During his years in office, he'd gained valuable experience working with lawmakers and overseeing the state's enormous budget. Now, he confronted a much greater task: directing the fortunes of the most powerful nation in the world. But if Reagan was nervous, he didn't show it. And neither did the trusted aides he brought with him from California. Many of Reagan's associates from his time

Shortly after taking office, President Reagan poses with Vice President George Bush (front right) and his cabinet.

as governor would play key roles in his presidential administration, helping him make important decisions. In the background, Nancy Reagan sometimes added her thoughts to conversations and plans, always wanting what was best for her husband.

This official portrait of Ronald Reagan was displayed in federal office buildings during his time as president.

The core California team was joined by a variety of other aides. Some shared Reagan's firm conservative views. Others were more moderate Republicans. With a few exceptions, most had not spent much time in government in Washington, D.C. For Jimmy Carter, that same lack of experience had led to conflicts with Congress. Reagan, however, was more skillful at getting along with his political foes. And compared to Carter, he had greater personal popularity and greater support for his plans.

The main themes of Reagan's campaign became the focus of his presidency. His top concern was reducing taxes and government spending. His second speech as president came on February 5, 1981, and addressed those issues. He told Americans openly that the country faced its worst economic problems since the Great Depression. To show the damaging

Help from the Stars?

Under Nancy's influence, Reagan sometimes looked to the stars for guidance. In California, both Reagans had been friendly with astrologers, people who believe the positions of the planets and stars influence human events. During Reagan's presidency, Nancy met regularly with an astrologer, and tried to arrange her husband's schedule to fit the predictions. Nancy often worried about Reagan's safety, and her goal was to protect him from anyone who wanted to do him harm.

effect of inflation, he held out a quarter, a dime, and a penny. A dollar from 1960 was now worth just that amount of change—36 cents. Reagan blamed inflation on the government's deficit. "It's time to recognize that we've come to a turning point . . ." he said. "And the old business-as-usual treatment can't save us." His solution: A 10 percent cut in taxes for all Americans for three years, plus cuts in the federal budget. Reagan's advisors called his plan "supply-side economics." Others began to call it "Reaganomics." Lowering taxes would give people more money to spend and invest. As they used their money this way, the economy would grow. But some Democrats doubted it would work—especially since Reagan also wanted to increase military spending by billions of dollars. Those competing desires meant that Reagan would find it almost impossible to reduce the deficit, as he said he would. To the critics, Reagan's plan was still voodoo economics.

For the first two months of Reagan's presidency, he tried to win support in Congress for his plans. Among his chief opponents was Tip O'Neill, the speaker of the House of Representatives, the most important post in that branch of Congress. At the time, the House was controlled by Democrats, and O'Neill was a traditional liberal who thought the government could solve most problems. Reagan disagreed, often asserting that government was the problem. Although O'Neill tried to stop Reagan's plans, some of his fellow Democrats backed the new president. O'Neill later summed up why fighting Reagan was so hard: "People like him as an individual . . . they want him to be a success." O'Neill also praised Reagan's skill in handling the media. He had spent his lifetime talking to people, expressing ideas in a simple way. He was, as many called him, "the Great Communicator."

The communication was not always public. Reagan answered his own mail, a rarity among modern presidents. He wrote to one voter, "You specified that you wanted to hear from me personally, so here I am." That personal touch made

Although they were political foes, Reagan liked Tip O'Neill personally and thought he was a good storyteller.

Chaos ensues after the attempted assassination of Ronald Reagan. Three other people were also injured during the shooting.

Americans feel that their president truly cared about them.

Another part of Reagan's appeal was his sense of humor. He never lost it, even when facing the toughest situations—something he proved on March 30, 1981. That day, he gave a speech at a Washington hotel and was walking back to his car when popping noises startled him. Reagan asked what the noises were, but the Secret Service agents around him knew. These men, specially trained to guard the president, pushed him into the waiting car. The pops were gunfire, and only later did Reagan realize that a sudden pain in his chest came from a bullet. His would-be killer, John Hinckley, Jr., was a disturbed man who had spent years drifting in and out of college. After the shooting, Hinckley was quickly arrested. He was later found innocent by reason of insanity and confined to a mental hospital.

Reagan later wrote in his diary about the shooting: "The car took off. I sat up on the edge of the seat almost paralyzed by pain. Then I began coughing up blood. . ." At the hospital, he learned the bullet was in his lung. On a rolling table, the president briefly passed out. For a moment, one of the Secret Service agents thought Reagan was dead. Soon Nancy arrived, and Reagan joked, "Honey, I forgot to duck." Later, as a doctor prepared to operate, Reagan joked again: "I hope you're a Republican." The doctor was not, but he told the president, "Today, we're all Republicans."

> **ASSASSINATION**
>
> An assassination is the deliberate killing of a single, usually important, person.

The surgery took almost three hours, but it was a success. Reagan had been lucky. The bullet had barely missed his heart. He lost half the blood in his body before the doctors closed the wound and gave him more blood. He spent almost two weeks in the hospital and then slowly finished recovering at home.

Although he certainly didn't enjoy being shot, the attempted assassination boosted Reagan's popularity.

Although up on his feet, Reagan was suffering from a high fever when this picture was taken, several days after the assassination attempt.

And it boosted his faith in God as well. He wrote, "Whatever happens now I owe my life to God and will try to serve him in any way I can." Reagan had always maintained a strong belief in God, though he was rarely outwardly religious. He didn't try to convince others to become Christians or condemn them if they sinned. Reagan welcomed the support of the religious right, but he didn't always actively pursue its political goals. His faith was more personal, and was now stronger than ever.

On April 28, Reagan spoke to the public for the first time since the shooting. He remained committed to his economic plan. That July, Congress approved the tax cuts and his budget plan, including a $26.4 billion increase in military spending. The total was more than Congress had ever approved for the United States military.

After leaving the hospital, Reagan returned to the White House, where he continued to receive close medical attention.

Although Reagan had tackled economic issues first, he didn't neglect foreign affairs. By this time, the Cold

War had entered a new phase. Détente seemed to be over, given Reagan's fierce anti-Communism. He believed Soviet leaders would "commit any crime" or undertake any deception to destroy capitalism. Reagan was not about to let that happen. Military plans that Jimmy Carter had approved and Reagan supported would put more nuclear weapons in Europe. Reagan later introduced new weapons systems. He also continued giving money and arms to Afghan rebels fighting the Soviet Union. For years, the United States had been bogged down in Vietnam. Now, the Russians were the ones facing a difficult foreign war, in Afghanistan. Reagan hoped to help the Afghans any way he could.

Reagan and his advisors also worried about the spread of Communism closer to home. Several countries in Latin America were battling Communist rebels, and Reagan sent

Nicaragua

For many years, the United States supported a dictator in Nicaragua named Anastasio Somoza. When he was forced from power in 1979, different parties competed to run the country. The struggle was won by a group called the Sandinistas, who set up a Soviet-style Communist government. Most of the non-Communists fled, while some formed a group called the "contras" to fight against Sandinista rule. Reagan wanted to prevent the Sandinistas from spreading Communism to other parts of Latin America.

aid to the governments of those nations. Meanwhile, in Nicaragua (another Latin-American nation), pro-Soviet forces known as the Sandinistas had already taken

power. In hopes of weakening their regime, Reagan sent support to anti-Sandinista rebels called contras. Some of the aid Reagan sent to Latin America would be covert—given secretly. But Reagan's plans for the region soon became public. They upset Democrats who knew that some of the people Reagan wanted to aid often brutally killed innocent civilians. Ultimately, the president would have a tough time winning support in Congress for his plans in Latin America.

As 1981 ended, the United States was in the middle of a recession. More people raised doubts about Reagan's economic plans—especially after his top economic advisor, David Stockman, seemed to have the same doubts. Stockman admitted he hadn't given Congress accurate numbers when discussing the budget plan. "None of us understands what's really going on with these numbers," Stockman said. Reagan admitted that in the future, he might have to ask for tax

In the fall of 1981, TV broadcaster Barbara Walters interviews Reagan at his ranch.

Reagan challenges Communism while speaking to Parliament, the lawmaking body of the British government.

increases to accomplish all his goals.

The economy remained bad through much of 1982, with 11 million people unemployed. At the same time, Reagan's budget cuts had reduced the money available for government aid programs. In meetings with lawmakers, Reagan sometimes didn't seem focused on the problems the country faced. He told stories not related to the topic at hand, and one reporter stated that there was a "a growing suspicion that the President has only a passing acquaintance with some of the most important decisions of his administration." But Reagan's closest aides said he still paid attention to the policies that mattered most to him— and Reagan still believed in his plan for the economy. He felt it just needed time to work.

Reagan was also still effective when speaking publicly. On June 8, 1982, he gave a speech in England that is now one of his most famous. Speaking to British lawmakers, Reagan talked about Communism and the Soviet Union. He praised workers in Poland who were resisting their Communist government, which was controlled by Moscow. He also said

TOTALITARIAN

Totalitarian describes a government that severely limits personal freedom.

that history proved an important fact: Free societies survive, and totalitarian states such as the Soviet Union do not. Communism, Reagan said, would end up on the "ash heap of history." And free countries, such as the United States, had to do all they could to promote democracy around the world.

Reagan was already trying to do that in Nicaragua by sending more aid to the contras. Congress opposed these efforts to topple the Communist Sandinistas. Some lawmakers also opposed Reagan's support for brutal anti-Communist leaders across Latin America. At the end of 1982, Congress passed a law preventing the U.S. government from sending secret aid to the contras.

Wreckage litters the street after the bombing of the U.S. embassy in Beirut, Lebanon, which killed 63 people.

In April 1983, Reagan planned to address Congress, looking for more money to aid friendly governments in Latin America. As he prepared his speech, he received jarring news: Terrorists had bombed the U.S. embassy in Beirut, Lebanon, in an area of southwest Asia known as the Middle East.

Reagan talks to a U.S. military commander in Beirut, as fighting continues in Lebanon.

This whole area had been filled with conflict for many years. Various terrorist groups, some based in Lebanon, clashed with Israel, the Americans' closest ally in the region. Meanwhile, Christians and Muslims in Lebanon fought over who should rule their nation. Earlier, Reagan had sent U.S. troops to Lebanon as part of an international peacekeeping force. When the terrorists attacked the U.S. embassy, they were protesting the presence of these troops and American support for Israel. Reagan called the attack cowardly but said the United States was prepared to stay in the region and work for peace.

The summer and fall of 1983 were difficult months for Reagan and the nation. The economy was improving, but world events continued to present dangers. On October 23, terrorists once again struck in Beirut, and this time they targeted American soldiers. A truck filled with explosives blew up in front of a military base, killing 241 U.S. servicemen, most of them marines. A second attack not

After the terrorist bombing of marine barracks in Beirut, U.S. forces faced continued fighting that killed or wounded dozens of troops.

far away killed 58 French peacekeepers. Reagan vowed that the United States wouldn't leave Lebanon until the troops finished their mission. He said, "Many Americans are wondering why we must keep our forces in Lebanon. Well, the reason they must stay there until the situation is under control is quite clear: We have vital interests in Lebanon, and our actions in Lebanon are in the cause of world peace . . . By promoting peace in Lebanon, we strengthen the forces for peace throughout the Middle East. This is not a Republican or a Democratic goal but one that all Americans share."

Reagan wanted to strike back at the terrorists, but some of his aides urged him to be cautious. They wanted to make sure a U.S. attack would not kill civilians. When American forces finally struck, the terrorist position was well defended, and the enemy shot down two U.S. planes.

By that time, however, Reagan and his staff could take pride in one military success. On October 22, the day before the second Beirut bombing, Reagan approved an invasion of the Caribbean island of Grenada. The Communist leader there had recently been murdered by a small group seeking power. Other island nations in the region urged Reagan to send in forces to restore order. Reagan was eager to do this: He had long feared that Grenada was being used by Cuba, a Soviet ally, to threaten U.S. interests. He was also told that American medical students on the island were in danger. Following Reagan's orders, a 7,000-member U.S. force invaded on October 25. They met some resistance from Cuban forces but quickly took control of the island.

The quick victory gave Reagan a boost in the polls, but it didn't soften the pain of the Beirut bombing and the failed U.S. mission there. Both Democrats and Republicans soon called for the U.S. troops to leave the area. They feared an even larger war, one that most Americans weren't ready to fight. Reagan agreed, and in February 1984 the troops came home. By then, Reagan was already in the middle of another battle—to win the 1984 presidential election.

Reagan makes an early-morning phone call to Vice President Bush regarding the developing situation in Grenada.

9

Four More Years

As 1984 began, readers of *Time* magazine saw Ronald Reagan and Soviet leader Yuri Andropov on the cover. The two men were shown standing back to back, suggesting the tense relationship between their two countries. Both sides feared the other could launch a nuclear attack. In the United States and Western Europe, many ordinary citizens also feared a war. Starting in 1982, hundreds of thousands of them had protested the continuing U.S. buildup of nuclear weapons.

One Reagan proposal particularly worried Andropov and others. On March 23, 1983, Reagan proposed a missile defense system that "could intercept and destroy . . . missiles before they reached our own soil

From the White House, President Reagan announces the SDI project. An article he read in 1981 helped fuel his interest in the plan.

or that of our allies." One of the proposed ways of doing this was to put powerful lasers on satellites that would orbit Earth. Those lasers, along with some on the ground, would shoot down missiles soon after they were launched.

Some activists condemned SDI, or "Star Wars," and demanded a ban on space-based weapons.

Years earlier, the United States and the Soviet Union had agreed not to build anti-missile defense systems. Many thought such systems could give one country the confidence to launch a surprise attack, knowing that missile defense would stop the other side's counterattack. Reagan disagreed with this view. He thought that a continual buildup of nuclear weapons, without any kind of defense system, would eventually lead to war.

Reagan's idea was called the Strategic Defense Initiative (SDI). Critics thought the technology would be too costly or not effective, and suggested that the defense system would do nothing but anger the Soviets, which it did. Some called the plan "Star Wars." But Reagan had a growing commitment to preventing the outbreak of nuclear war. He later wrote, "Even if a nuclear war did not mean the extinction of mankind, it would certainly mean the end of civilization as we knew it. No one could 'win' a nuclear war."

Reagan knew his tough talk sometimes upset the Russians. It also worried some Americans. As he prepared for the 1984 presidential election, Reagan tried to calm their fears. He talked more about his desire to get rid of nuclear weapons. Still, he told voters and the world that the United States would continue to increase its overall military strength.

The Reagan administration's willingness to use military might against Communism soon became clear in Nicaragua. Early in 1984, a Soviet ship hit a mine in a Nicaraguan port. The mine had been secretly placed there by the Central Intelligence Agency (CIA), the main U.S. spy agency. Even some Republicans reacted angrily when they heard the news. Senator Barry Goldwater wrote, "This is an act violating international law. It is an act of war." Congress and the American public had

Reagan supported the contras of Nicaragua, comparing them to the Americans who fought for independence from Great Britain.

largely resisted Reagan's efforts to wage a covert war in Latin America, but he remained concerned about events there. Despite the resistance, his administration continued to aid the contras.

As his reelection campaign gathered steam, Reagan had several factors on his side. The most important was the economy, which had come roaring back after the recession of his early presidency—seven million jobs were created in 1984. He was also helped by an outburst of patriotism, centered around the

Prayer in the Classroom

During the 1980s, school prayer was a major issue for the religious right in America. Earlier, the Supreme Court had outlawed most prayer in public schools. The Court said it violated the First Amendment of the Constitution, which prevents the government from promoting religion or favoring one faith over another. Reagan supported a new amendment to the Constitution that would allow voluntary school prayer, spoken out loud, as opposed to the silent prayer others thought might be allowable. The amendment was never approved.

Olympics, which were held in Los Angeles that year.

Yet a number of Americans opposed Reagan and his policies. His administration sometimes ignored laws intended to protect the environment. And several officials had to leave their jobs because they had committed crimes or were accused of unethical acts. On the whole, though, Americans focused on the positive side of Reagan and his presidency. They welcomed his charm and optimism. They felt a renewed pride in being Americans after the struggles of Vietnam, Watergate, and the Iranian hostage crisis. Reagan helped remind them by running ads that said, "It's morning again in America . . . families can have confidence again in the future. America today is prouder and stronger and better."

That summer, the Democrats chose Walter Mondale as their presidential candidate. He had served as vice president under President Carter. To some Americans, Mondale was a reminder of a difficult time they preferred to forget. The two candidates met in several debates. Mondale accused Reagan of not being in charge of the government or knowing the facts needed to defend the country. But nothing Mondale or others said really hurt Reagan's popularity.

The Reagans greet the crowd at the 1984 Republican Convention, held in San Diego, California. Barry Goldwater was one of the speakers.

For many years, the United States sent military aid to the mujahideen, Afghan Muslims fighting the Soviet Union.

With the recession past and the nation at peace, most Americans really did feel like they were better off than they had been four years earlier.

Mondale tried to gain support by choosing Geraldine Ferraro as his running mate. She was the first woman ever nominated for vice president by a major U.S. party. But the choice didn't help the Democrats. On election day, November 6, Reagan scored the largest presidential victory in U.S. history. Mondale won just his home state of Minnesota and the District of Columbia. Reagan later wrote, "I saw the election as approval of what I'd been trying to do and a mandate to continue it." But Tip O'Neill and other Democrats had other plans. Reagan would find them less willing to work with him during the next four years.

Still, Reagan was able to accomplish many of his goals, sometimes without support from Congress. Overseas, he increased aid to the mujahideen, the Afghan Muslims battling the Soviet Union. Thanks to previous U.S. aid, the mujahideen had kept the Soviets from extending control over large parts of Afghanistan. Reagan also sought to give more aid to the contras. Despite the new law barring such aid, his administration was still secretly sending money and weapons to the Nicaraguan rebels. In reference to the contras, Reagan had told one of his top aides, Bud McFarlane, "I want you to do whatever you have to do to help them keep body and soul together." Reagan's secretary of state, George Shultz, worried the president might be pursuing a goal that could lead to impeachment. Still, McFarlane and his aides kept looking for secret ways to help the contras.

Reagan also moved to improve relations with Iraq, a Middle Eastern nation that had been fighting a war with Iran for several years. Like the terrorists in Lebanon, Iran was still hostile toward the United States and Israel. Although Reagan claimed publicly that America was neutral in the Iran-Iraq War, he had been secretly aiding Iraqi leader Saddam Hussein.

Finally, Reagan was still eager to reduce nuclear weapons. Earlier, he had called the Soviet Union an "evil empire,"

and most conservatives completely agreed. Many were surprised—and uneasy—when Reagan talked more and more about negotiating with the Soviets on nuclear arms.

Funding for SDI led to work on this high-energy laser. The United States is still pursuing anti-missile defense systems but has not launched any space-based lasers.

As it happened, the Soviet Union also seemed more interested in talks. American reporters thought their fear of SDI had made the Russians more willing to meet with Reagan. Soviet leaders later denied this, but at least one Russian leader knew the country was reaching a turning point. Mikhail Gorbachev took over as leader of the Soviet Communist Party in March 1985. He would play a key role in improving Soviet relations with the United States.

Throughout his presidency, Reagan had puzzled Soviet leaders. He

Mikhail Gorbachev

As a young man, Mikhail Gorbachev accepted the values of the Communist Party. But later, as he traveled to other countries, his views started to change. After becoming the Soviet leader in 1984, he began two important programs. One, called *perestroika,* involved reforming the nation's strict Communist economy. The other, called *glasnost,* focused on giving the Soviet people more freedom and contact with the outside world. His policies helped end Communist rule in the Soviet Union and across Eastern Europe.

talked of destroying Communism and confronting the Russians around the world. Yet he also seemed willing to reduce nuclear weapons and sent private messages to Soviet leaders, trying to arrange meetings. But the Soviet Union during the early 1980s had three different leaders, all old and sickly men who died in office. When Gorbachev came to power, he was much younger and willing to discuss new ideas. Reagan saw that Gorbachev might finally be a Russian leader he could work with in a constructive way.

Soon after Gorbachev took power, George Shultz visited him in Moscow. Shultz brought with him a message from Reagan: "President Reagan told me to look you squarely in the eyes and tell you: 'Ronald Reagan believes this is a very special moment in the history of mankind.'" American and Russian officials were already meeting in Geneva, Switzerland, to discuss arms cuts. Reagan thought the time was right for Gorbachev and him to meet directly. As the two leaders exchanged letters, Reagan could see that Gorbachev was smart and wouldn't give in easily to American demands. But he believed the two countries shared common ground. He told Gorbachev, "I would hope that this common ground can be expanded." Reagan added, "I will personally spare no effort to bring this about."

Reagan holds a "Tax Ax," meant to show his willingness to cut taxes again during his second term.

Before meeting with Gorbachev, Reagan dealt with a number of other issues. He battled with Congress on sending non-military aid to the contras, with the lawmakers killing his proposal. He also pushed for a major change in tax

Reagan meets Mikhail Gorbachev for the first time. Their planned 15-minute meeting lasted for almost an hour.

rates, which determined how much people paid, based on their income. He called the plan the "second American Revolution." This led to the Tax Reform Act of 1986, which was also supported by key Democrats. Under the new law, several million people with low incomes paid no taxes, while companies paid more. Experts called the tax changes the most important domestic act of Reagan's second term.

The tax changes, however, did not have the worldwide impact that Reagan's relationship with Gorbachev did. The two men held their first meeting in November 1985 in Geneva. As the leader of the Soviet Union, Gorbachev wanted Communism to survive. But the military rivalry between his country and the United States was dangerous for the world. Reagan had come to this same conclusion, so he and Gorbachev did share an important "common ground." In addition, the arms race kept the Soviets from spending money on their own people. Gorbachev was ready for a change.

Reagan still distrusted the Soviets and their aims around the world. He wanted Gorbachev to stop Soviet efforts to spread Communism. But his personal distrust of the Soviet leader began to melt after they finally met. "There was something likable about Gorbachev. There was warmth in his face and

his style . . ." But Reagan planned to follow an old Russian saying: *Dovorey no provorey*—"trust, but verify." On

Meeting in Geneva, Reagan and Gorbachev spent some of their time together sharing jokes and personal stories.

any deal he might make, the president wanted to be sure the Russians really did whatever they promised to do.

The two men disagreed about SDI. Reagan was thinking that the Americans could share their new technology with the Soviet Union. Gorbachev couldn't see the point of spreading the arms race into space. As the talks went on, Reagan impressed Gorbachev and his advisors. They had heard the president was an elderly man who sometimes seemed to have trouble following conversations. On the topics he cared most about, though, Reagan was sharp and in control. SDI was one of these topics. So was his call for improving human rights in the Soviet Union.

When the summit ended, the two leaders had a general agreement to reduce their nuclear weapons by 50 percent. The details, however, were far from worked out. They also said they would continue to talk about weapons in space. Reagan said he had met with Gorbachev to seek "a fresh start in relations between the United States and the Soviet Union . . . I'm convinced that we're heading in the right direction." The two leaders agreed to meet again in Washington.

Before that summit was arranged, Gorbachev wanted one more meeting with Reagan at a neutral site. In October 1986, the two men met in Reykjavik, Iceland, in a historic building called Höfdi House. The Soviets and Americans had been holding talks during the time between the two summits, but the negotiations had not brought the progress Gorbachev wanted. The Reykjavik meeting led to the bold call by both men to eliminate all nuclear weapons. Once again, SDI remained the issue that kept the two countries apart. But Reagan and Gorbachev had given the world hope that the risk of nuclear war might be greatly reduced, and the two governments would continue to hold important discussions. In general, Americans approved of Reagan's talks with Gorbachev, and many were convinced he would make a major arms agreement that would end the era of Cold War hostilities once and for all.

Höfdi House in Reykjavik, Iceland, was the scene of the second meeting between Reagan and Gorbachev.

chapter **10**

Iran, Contras, and the President

On Reagan's first day as president in 1981, the Iranian hostage crisis had come to an end. But the release of the hostages didn't improve relations between the United States and Iran. And it didn't end the kidnapping of Americans in the Middle

In May 1985, Lebanese terrorists released these photos of six hostages. William Buckley, top center, worked for the CIA and was killed by his kidnappers.

East. During the first few years of Reagan's presidency, terrorist groups with ties to Iran seized seven Americans in Lebanon.

At the same time, Iran was still fighting its long war with Iraq. A U.S. law prohibited the selling of weapons to either side. By 1985, however, the Iranians were desperate for arms. So desperate, they secretly asked for a trade— U.S. weapons in exchange for the release of the American hostages.

Reagan liked the idea, since he was concerned about the safety of the American hostages. The first of two arms shipments reached Iran through Israel in August 1985. But the Iranians did not keep their side of the bargain. They released just one of the seven hostages. Administration officials continued to talk with the Israelis and Iranians. In November, Reagan noted in his diary, "It is a complex undertaking with only a few of us in on it. I won't even write in the diary what we're up to."

The war between Iran and Iraq, which lasted almost eight years, resulted in at least one million casualties.

Reagan had always opposed dealing with terrorists to win the release of the Americans. But Reagan believed he was negotiating with Iranians who opposed the harsh rule of Ayatollah Khomeini. He told aides flatly, "We're not dealing

A sign in Nicaragua celebrates the capture of Eugene Hasenfus, an American who revealed details about secret U.S. aid to the contras.

with terrorists." Later, however, it was learned that the Iranians Reagan's aides spoke to really were linked to the Khomeini regime.

On December 5, 1985, Reagan signed a paper approving all the arms deals so far and any to come. Several times in 1986, the Americans sent more missiles to Iran. Finally, later in the year, the terrorists released several Americans. But just as quickly, the terrorists seized new hostages. Through all this, neither Congress nor the U.S. public knew about the deal.

By this time, the Iranian arms sales had become linked to events in another part of the world. Lieutenant Colonel Oliver North of the National Security Council had followed Reagan's request to keep funding the military efforts of the contras in Nicaragua. With the Iranian arms deal, North saw a new way to do this. He took some of the money Iran paid the United States and used it to buy weapons for the contras. As with most previous shipments, the supplies were sent secretly.

The details of the two secret deals finally emerged in the fall of 1986. That October, Nicaragua shot down a U.S. plane operated by the CIA. One of the crew members, an American, survived the crash. He told the Nicaraguans about

the secret aid for the contras. Reagan later told reporters, "There is no U.S. government connection with that at all."

Starting the next month, reports appeared about U.S. arm sales to Iran meant to help free American hostages. On November 13, Reagan went on TV to give his version of the facts: "I authorized the transfer of small amounts of defensive weapons and spare parts for defensive systems to Iran….These modest deliveries, taken together, could easily fit into a single cargo plane." Reagan insisted the deal was meant to improve relations with Iran, along with perhaps freeing the hostages. But it was not a direct swap.

However, the document Reagan had signed in December 1985 admitted there was a direct swap. He was also wrong about the weapons. They included several thousand missiles designed to destroy tanks and were

Reagan meets with (left to right) Caspar Weinberger, George Shultz, Ed Meese, and Don Regan to discuss the Iran-contra affair.

not strictly for Iran's defense. Polls soon showed that few Americans liked Reagan's Iran policy. And many thought the president was lying to them.

Soon, Ed Meese, the U.S. attorney general, revealed the last piece of the Iran-contra puzzle: Some of the proceeds from the Iranian arms deal had been used to help the contras. Reagan insisted he didn't know about the funding

As Iran-contra unfolded, the Reagans limited their contact with reporters and the public.

of the contras with Iranian money. North and his boss, Admiral John Poindexter, said that the complex operation had been carried out without Reagan's knowledge, but critics of the administration were skeptical of their claims.

Reagan knew he had to respond to the growing questions and criticisms. He set up a group called the Tower Commission to investigate the National Security Council's actions. Meanwhile, Congress prepared for its own investigations, since many lawmakers sensed that Reagan had acted unwisely, if not illegally.

Through 1987, various committees gathered details about the affair. During this

ATTORNEY GENERAL

An attorney general is the chief lawyer for a state or national government.

time, Reagan limited his public appearances. Some of this was tied to health issues—he had minor surgery in January. But mostly, his advisors wanted him to avoid questions about the Iran-contra events. When the first Congressional committee report appeared, it said that the Iran deal was a swap of arms for hostages and that Reagan had approved almost all the details. The report also said that members of the administration had lied to Congress and other government officials about the deal.

In February, Reagan appeared before the Tower Commission. For a man so used to public speaking and performing, he wasn't at ease. In a summary of the commission's final report, the *New York Times* stated that the group saw Reagan "as a confused and remote figure who failed to understand or control the secret arms

Here, Reagan meets with members of the Tower Commission for the second time, changing some of his previous statements.

deal with Iran, and who thus had to 'take responsibility' for a policy that in the end caused 'chaos' at home and embarrassment abroad."

Reagan helped his cause on March 14, 1987, when he gave a speech admitting he had made a mistake. He had been wrong when he first described the details of the arms-for-hostages deal, and he acknowledged that: "Now, what should happen when you make a mistake is this: You take your knocks, you learn your lessons, and then you move on. That's the healthiest way to deal with a problem."

If many Americans thought the president had lied back in November, more now believed he meant what he said—and were ready to forgive him. Reagan's approval rating went up by nine points in a poll taken after the speech.

Still the Iran-contra scandal would not go away. For several months during the summer, Congress questioned North, Poindexter, and others. The hearings were televised, giving Americans a chance to hear North talk about his destruction of documents relating to the contras. In the end, Congress couldn't find any evidence that challenged what Reagan had said—he didn't know the Iranian money was used to

Oliver North describes his efforts to help the contras. To some Americans, North was a hero for providing aid, even if he broke the law.

help the contras. Still, Reagan felt responsible for all that had happened. In an August speech he said, "The fact of the matter is that there's nothing I can say that will make the situation right. I was stubborn in my pursuit of a policy that went astray."

In the early days of the scandal, some of Reagan's aides worried he might be impeached. He seemed more concerned about losing the trust of the American people. One poll taken after the August speech showed half of Americans still thought Reagan had lied about his role in Iran-contra. But that number was down from just a

The Last Report

In December 1986, the U.S. government chose attorney Lawrence Walsh to determine whether anyone broke the law during the Iran-contra affair. Walsh collected evidence for more than four years. He found that about a dozen people had broken the law. Several were tried and found guilty. Walsh's final report was released in 1993, and confirmed what Reagan had said all along: There was no believable evidence that Reagan knew about the use of money from the Iranian arms deals to help the contras. But Walsh also wrote that Reagan "created the conditions which made possible the crimes committed by others." In 1992, President George Bush pardoned several of the people found guilty during the scandal.

few months before. Slowly but surely, Reagan was gaining back the people's trust. Many still supported him and his policies, even if he had made mistakes as president. Soon, the public outcries over the Iran-contra affair died down, and Reagan's reputation continued to recover.

chapter

11
End of a Presidency

As the Iran-contra investigations went on, President Reagan tried to stay focused on his job. He worked for his usual goals of reducing the size of the government and lowering taxes. He also called for more money to enforce laws and stop the flow of illegal drugs. Over the course of 1987, Reagan lost some battles with Congress. The Senate rejected his choice of Robert Bork to fill an empty seat on the U.S. Supreme Court. Under the Constitution, the Senate must approve all federal judges named by the president. Democratic senators thought Bork was too conservative.

As his presidency neared its end, Reagan continued to work. In June 1988, he learned unemployment had hit a 14-year low.

They charged that he had opposed past legal efforts to give African-Americans equal rights and didn't believe that the Constitution gave Americans a right to privacy.

Despite the Bork incident and the Iran-contra investigations, Reagan could point with pride to many accomplishments in 1987. The economy as a whole was still strong, compared to the bad years earlier in the decade. Inflation remained low, and companies had created about 18 million new jobs during Reagan's presidency. His policies had cut taxes for everyone, and most middle-class Americans had seen their incomes rise.

Robert Bork's failure to win support in the Senate led to a new term: To be "borked" now means to be attacked for holding extreme views.

Still, not all of Reagan's economic goals had been met. The debt had soared, mostly because Reagan and Congress had kept spending, even though there was less money coming in. The country was also facing a banking crisis: Many organizations called savings and loans (which functioned much like banks) had collapsed after making bad investments, costing taxpayers billions of dollars.

Meanwhile, Reagan was still actively pursuing good relations with the Soviet Union. After the Reykjavik meeting, the two sides continued to discuss the reduction of nuclear

At a speech in Berlin, Germany, in June 1987, Reagan tells a crowd of people that the Berlin Wall should come down.

weapons. Mikhail Gorbachev said each country should get rid of all their intermediate-range nuclear weapons (known as INF) in Europe. The Soviet leader was ready to do this, no matter what the United States did with Star Wars. Reagan agreed, and talks went on for months to work out the details. Reagan then sent George Shultz to Moscow with a message: If Gorbachev wanted even better relations, he should pull Soviet troops out of Afghanistan and reduce his support of Communists in Latin America.

In fact, Reagan's policies had already played a key role in shaping events in Afghanistan. The administration had sent potent Stinger missiles to the Afghan rebels. The missiles were used to shoot down low-flying Soviet planes and helicopters.

The aircraft were thus forced to fly at higher altitudes, where they were less effective. The Soviets could only control small parts of the country. As a result, Gorbachev was forced to consider getting out of Afghanistan sooner rather than later.

In June, Reagan traveled to Germany to deliver a spoken challenge to Gorbachev. For decades, the Berlin Wall had split the city of Berlin in two. On the west side was a democratic government loyal to the United States. On the east was a strict Communist government with strong ties to the Soviet Union. Germany itself was also divided this way. Standing before the wall in West Berlin, Reagan said, "General Secretary Gorbachev, if you seek peace, if you seek prosperity for the Soviet Union and Eastern Europe, if you seek liberalization: Come here to this gate! Mr. Gorbachev, open this gate! Mr. Gorbachev, tear down this wall!"

Gorbachev was not ready to tear down the Berlin Wall,

The Berlin Wall

The wall snaking across Berlin was one of the most famous symbols of the Cold War. It represented the deep divide in beliefs between democratic and Communist nations. East Germany, with Soviet permission, had built the wall in 1961. The East Germans wanted to keep their citizens from fleeing the country, seeking freedom in West Berlin or other parts of Europe. This didn't stop people from trying to sneak over the wall, however, and many of them died in the attempt.

Reagan and Gorbachev sign the INF treaty. Several days before, Gorbachev said on American television that his country and the United States should be allies.

but he was willing to come to the United States for another face-to-face meeting with Reagan. The two leaders met on December 8, 1987, to sign a treaty getting rid of INF weapons. They also agreed to reduce the number of long-range missiles each country owned by 50 percent. At the treaty signing, Reagan noted the importance of the event, and the changes in attitude that had occured since he took office. "For the first time in history, the language of 'arms control' was replaced by 'arms reduction'—in this case, the complete elimination of an entire class of U.S. and Soviet nuclear missiles." Reagan hoped it was just the beginning of more cuts and a deeper Soviet-American friendship. In another good sign, Gorbachev soon announced he would pull all Soviet troops out of Afghanistan.

The meetings between Reagan and Gorbachev had gone well. The two men had made history together, and they also got along with each other as people. They genuinely liked each other. And the American public, on the whole, still liked Reagan. Opinion polls gave him positive ratings, compared to the worst days of Iran-contra. But few people outside the White House saw how hard it was for the 77-year-old president to run the country effectively.

Old age had magnified some of Reagan's previous weaknesses. His hearing had gotten a little worse, and at times he forgot names and facts. Yet at other times, he was as sharp and energetic as ever, especially in his last meetings with Gorbachev. Although he may have slowed down a little, Reagan could still impress others with his skill.

Reagan had never won many friends among liberals. By his last year as president, even some conservatives thought he had made mistakes. They still did not trust the Soviet Union, and they disliked the arms reductions Reagan made. (Many had tried to block the INF treaty.) Some conservatives also thought he had not done enough to shrink the size of government. During Reagan's time in office, the number of civilian workers in the federal government had actually gone up by 150,000. Social conservatives, especially the religious right, also thought Reagan should have done

This and other Soviet SS-23 missiles were among those set to be destroyed under the terms of the INF treaty.

While visiting Moscow's historic Red Square, Reagan shakes hands with a young Russian.

more to fight the practice of abortion and push Christian values.

One Christian minister who did support Reagan was Pat Robertson. Seeking to put the country on an even more conservative path, he ran for the Republican presidential nomination in 1988. So did several other candidates, including Vice President George Bush. Reagan and Bush had not been personally close during the eight years they served together, but Reagan supported Bush in his race for the presidency. At one point, he told Bush to "go out there and win one for the Gipper."

As the presidential campaign unfolded, Reagan made his last important overseas trip. In May 1988, for the first time, he visited Moscow. Gorbachev was ready to discuss more arms cuts, but Reagan was more interested in the rights of Soviet citizens. He said they should be able to freely practice their religion. After the meeting, Reagan briefly stepped out of his car to shake hands with average Russians on the street. Amazed, the people crowded around him, cheering as Reagan walked. Then Soviet police quickly moved in to keep them away. Reagan was stunned to see innocent, friendly people treated so badly. Despite Gorbachev's reforms, Reagan wrote in his diary, "some things haven't changed." But Reagan himself had changed a bit. A reporter asked if he thought he was in a country that was still an "evil empire." The president said no, adding, "I was talking about another time in another era."

Back in the United States, Reagan's era as president was almost over. He attended the Republican National Convention that summer as George Bush was nominated as the party's candidate. In the general election, Bush would face Governor Michael Dukakis of Massachusetts. Reagan worked hard for Bush during the fall campaign, eager to see him defeat the more-liberal Dukakis. He knew the Democrat would carry on few of his programs. Bush was more likely to keep them.

That November, Bush won an easy victory, and Reagan set up a team to help Bush prepare for his presidency. Reagan would be president for only a few more weeks. His years in the White House were coming to an end.

Reagan announces his support for George Bush's run for the White House in 1988. Bush easily won the Republican nomination.

chapter **12**

Last Years

During his last days as president, Ronald Reagan still had work to do. He met with foreign leaders. He received bills from Congress to sign into law and prepared one last federal budget. And in December, he visited one more time with his friend "Gorby," Mikhail Gorbachev. During this trip to the United States, the Soviet leader surprised many people once again. He said his country would withdraw troops from Eastern Europe and shrink its military at home.

Through December and into the new year, Reagan worked on his Farewell Address—

The Reagans pose for one of their last photos at the White House, just one month before the 1988 election.

the last speech he would give as president. He delivered it on January 11, 1989. He talked about his "two triumphs, two things that I'm proudest of. One is the economic recovery, in which the people of America created—and filled—19 million new jobs. The other is the recovery of our morale: America is respected again in the world, and looked to for leadership."

Reagan left the White House as one of the most popular presidents in modern times.

Reagan had kept a diary throughout his presidency. The last line for January 19 read, "Tomorrow I stop being president." The next day was sunny and chilly in Washington, D.C. The Reagans hosted the Bushes at the White House before George Bush was sworn in as president. When the ceremony was over, Ronald and Nancy Reagan boarded a helicopter, the first leg of their journey back to California. As Reagan left the White House, Americans had a high opinion of him and his presidency. Polls showed that 70 percent of the people approved of him.

During Reagan's presidency, he and Nancy had spent many vacations at their sprawling California ranch. Reagan now would have plenty of time there to ride his beloved horses. At times, he drove over the hundreds of acres in a Jeep with license plates that read "GIPPER." At other times, the Reagans lived in Bel Air, a wealthy neighborhood in Los Angeles.

Reagan also had an office in Los Angeles, where he worked on a new autobiography, *An American Life.*

Although he was no longer a part of the government, Reagan was still interested in politics and eager to promote conservative ideas. During 1990, he gave speeches supporting Republican candidates for various offices. He also raised money for a presidential library that was to be built in his honor in California.

By that time, the world had watched with amazement as one of Reagan's dreams came true: On November 9, 1989, the Berlin Wall was opened, allowing free travel between East and West Germany. Soon, German residents on both sides began the hard and joyous work of tearing down the wall.

Television viewers around the world watched as Germans celebrated, and worked to tear down the Berlin Wall.

The historic events came after months of change in Eastern Europe. Mikhail Gorbachev had given Eastern European nations under Soviet control their freedom. Soon, democratic governments would appear across the region. The Soviet Union also had its first free elections in decades. By the end of 1991, the Soviet Union no longer existed; it broke up into 15 separate countries.

These changes marked the end of the Cold War. Although they happened during the Bush presidency, Reagan received praise for ending the war. His willingness to reduce nuclear arms and deal openly with an "evil empire" were key factors. So was his determination to spend as much as possible to strengthen the U.S. military. On the other side, Gorbachev also won praise. Together, these two leaders overcame old attitudes and fears that could have locked the United States and the

The Ronald Reagan Presidential Library

In 1991, the Ronald Reagan Presidential Library and Museum opened in Simi Valley, California. Money for the building came from private donations. Five presidents attended its opening—Nixon, Ford, Carter, Reagan, and Bush. That marked the first time so many U.S. presidents had gathered at one occasion. The library holds the records from Reagan's time in office, and the museum contains various exhibits. One exhibit features a piece of the Berlin Wall, while another is a life-sized model of the Oval Office, as it was used by Reagan as president.

Speaking to Republicans at their 1992 convention, Reagan praised the peace and economic strength Americans enjoyed.

Soviet Union in conflict for decades. In 1992, Reagan attended the Republican National Convention. He talked about the end of the Cold War, and the role he and his administration had played: "We stood tall and proclaimed that Communism was destined for the ash heap of history . . . We knew then what the liberal Democrat leaders just couldn't figure out: the sky would not fall if America restored her strength and resolve. The sky would not fall if an American president spoke the truth. The only thing that would fall was the Berlin Wall."

A few months later, in March 1993, Reagan spoke about SDI. He had announced his plans for the missile-defense system 10 years earlier, and remained convinced the system could prevent an attack by the largest nuclear missiles. Even though the Cold War was over, Reagan saw other threats facing the nation. Other countries wanted nuclear weapons, and not all of them were friendly with the United States. Today, the original plan for SDI has been scrapped, but U.S. leaders still hope to build anti-missile defenses.

The SDI statement was one of the last Reagan made on important political issues. That same year, doctors found that

Reagan was suffering from Alzheimer's disease, an illness that destroys a person's memory and ability to do simple tasks. As of yet, there is no cure. In 1994, Reagan issued a personal statement, telling the world about his condition. In the past, he and Nancy had been open about battles with cancer. Now Reagan wanted to share the news about his Alzheimer's. He hoped "it might promote greater awareness of this condition. Perhaps it will encourage a greater understanding of the individuals and families affected by it."

Reagan said in his letter that he wanted to continue doing the things he loved. But soon, he could no longer ride horses on the ranch. His memory got worse, and Nancy had to take care of him.

Mikhail and Raisa Gorbachev spend time at the Reagans' ranch in 1992, just months after the collapse of the Soviet Union.

President George W. Bush (son of the first President Bush) was among the many world leaders who honored Reagan at his funeral in Washington, D.C.

But at times Reagan still went out, taking short walks at a local park. Occasionally, people approached the former president to say hello or have their picture taken.

During one walk in 1997, a boy and his grandfather approached Reagan. The grandfather was originally from Ukraine, a country that had won its independence after the collapse of Communism in the Soviet Union. The boy wanted his picture taken with Reagan, and Reagan agreed. As the boy and his grandfather left, the elderly man thanked Reagan for having fought Communism. Reagan simply said that it had been his job.

By 2000, Reagan's Alzheimer's had worsened. For the next four years, he lived but never opened his eyes. Finally, on June 5, 2004, Reagan died at his home in Bel Air. For a week, the nation mourned one of its most popular and controversial presidents. Conservatives praised him, with some forgetting the times when they thought Reagan had not been conservative enough. Liberals used kind words to describe his positive traits. Many though, still remembered their battles with the president on certain issues, such as Iran-contra and the budget.

Judging the achievements of a president is never easy. But over time, a general picture of Reagan and his presidency have emerged. His greatest success was working with Gorbachev to help end the Cold War. His greatest failure was probably Iran-contra—not just the specifics of the affair, but what they represented. Because he always focused his attention on the big picture, rather than on the details of his policies, Reagan too often left important decisions to his aides.

Reagan had a personal confidence and charm that helped boost the spirits of Americans during difficult times. He also forced many voters to consider what role the government should play in everyday life. Eventually, even many Democrats began to see the value of a smaller government. In this way, Reagan framed the political debate of the 1980s and beyond. Today, Ronald Reagan continues to be a symbol of optimism and freedom for many Americans. By running for president, this Hollywood movie star had taken on his most important and memorable role.

President Ronald Reagan continues to be a hero for many Americans, representing ideals of optimism and freedom.

Events in the Life of Ronald Reagan

1942–1945
During World War II,
Reagan serves in the U.S.
Army, making training films.

January 3, 1967
After a long and
successful election
campaign, Reagan is
sworn in as governor
of California.

February 6, 1911
Ronald Reagan is born, the
second son of Jack and Nelle
Reagan of Tampico, Illinois.

1932
Reagan graduates
from Eureka College
and finds work as a
radio announcer.

September 1954
Reagan becomes the host
of *General Electric Theater*
and soon begins making
speeches for GE.

January 1975
Reagan begins writi
a weekly news colu
and giving short, da
radio addresses.

Mid 1920s
Reagan goes to high
school in Dixon,
Illinois, where he wins
fame as a lifeguard.

October 1947
Reagan appears
before a Congressional
committee investigating
the influence of
Communists in
Hollywood.

October 27, 1964
Reagan wins national
attention with a
speech supporting
Republican
presidential candidate
Barry Goldwater.

August 19, 1976
Gerald Ford
defeats Reagan
in a close race for
the Republican
presidential
nomination.

June 1937
Reagan begins his successful
career as a Hollywood actor.

March 4, 1952
Reagan marries
Nancy Davis.

November 4, 1980
Reagan defeats Jimmy Carter to become the 40th president of the United States.

December 8, 1987
Reagan and Gorbachev sign the INF Treaty, eliminating a whole class of nuclear weapons.

February 1987
Reagan appears before a committee investigating the Iran-contra affair.

January 11, 1989
Reagan delivers his Farewell Address, at the end of his presidency.

March 23, 1983
Reagan introduces the idea of a space-based missile defense system called the Strategic Defense Initiative.

DEMILITARIZE SPACE
NO STAR WARS

November 5, 1994
Reagan announces he has Alzheimer's Disease.

November 6, 1984
Reagan easily defeats Walter Mondale to win a second term as president.

November 1985
Reagan meets with Soviet leader Mikhail Gorbachev to discuss cuts in the number of nuclear weapons.

June 5, 2004
Ronald Reagan dies at his home in Bel Air, California.

April 18, 1983
Terrorists bomb the U.S. Embassy in Beirut, Lebanon; an attack on U.S. Marines follows in October.

August 1985
U.S. arms reach Iran, part of a secret deal to trade weapons for the release of U.S. hostages held in Lebanon.

March 30, 1981
Reagan survives an assassination attempt.

For Further Study

If you're interested in reading about Ronald Reagan's life in his own words, his 1990 book *An American Life* is the most complete source.

An excellent online source for the highlights of Reagan's life and presidency is the Ronald Reagan Presidential Foundation and Library, at www.reaganlibrary.com. You can visit the library in person in Simi Valley, California.

For an overview of the Cold War, see the online exhibits of the Cold War Museum, at www.coldwar.org.

The University of California at Santa Barbara offers the American Presidency Project, a website with documents from every presidency and transcripts of key speeches and broadcasts of the modern presidents, including Reagan: www.presidency.ucsb.edu.

Ronald Reagan: the Great Communicator is a two-disc DVD with almost eight hours of footage on Reagan and his presidency. The set includes clips from his Hollywood career and highlights of his most famous speeches.

Works Cited

p.7 "It would be fine…" *The Role of a Lifetime*, 689; p.8 "The meeting is over…" *An American Life*, 679; p.11 "The gift of blarney…" *ibid.*, 21; p.11 "Always expected to find…" *ibid.*, 22; p.12 "God has a plan…" *ibid.*, 20; p.13 "I liked that approval…" *ibid.*, 35; p.14 "'Dutch' Reagan Has Made…" *Reagan's America*, 31; p.15 "He was the biggest mouth…" *ibid.*, 48; p.16 "For the first time in my life…" *An American Life*, 48; p.19 "Strong, gentle, confident voice…" *ibid.*, 66; p.20 "Theater of the mind," *ibid.*, 73; p.22 "As a result, I could hardly see… *ibid.*, 79; p.23 "You know, maybe I can make it here," *ibid.*, 86; p.25 "Win one for the Gipper," *ibid.*, 92; p.29 "Ghastly images, images on my mind…" *ibid.*, 99; p.34 "Attempted to be a disruptive influence…" House Un-American Activities Committee Testimony; p.38 "Mashed potato circuit," *Reagan, In His Own Hand*, 18; p.40 "The ever-expanding federal government…" *An American Life*, 129; p.41 "Whether we admit it or not…" *Ronald Reagan*, 75; p.44 "I'd do anything…" *An American Life*, 139; p.44 "Plan our lives for us," *The Public Papers of President Ronald W. Reagan*; p.45 "Well, perhaps there is a simple answer…" *ibid.*; p.46 "I had a good job…" *An American Life*, 145; p.48 "I am an ordinary citizen…" *Ronald Reagan*, 92; p.50 "An aging actor," *ibid.*, 94; p.53 "I just didn't think…" "Reagan," *American Experience*; p.54 "I realized I was going to need more time…" *An American Life*, 184; p.55 "A world of unreality," "Governor Reagan and California Welfare Reform," p.284; p.61 "Of the greatness of our people…" *ibid.*, 236; p.63 "The most feathers possible…" *ibid.*, 278; p.63 "Could find itself isolated in a hostile world…" *ibid.*, 113; p.64 "Crisis of confidence," "Jimmy Carter," *American Experience*; p.65 "Reduced to bickering…" Ronald Reagan Official Announcement, November 13, 1979; p.68 "I had always liked him personally…" *An American Life*, 216; p.69 "America had lost faith in itself… recapture our dreams…" *ibid.*, 219; p.69 "There you go again….Are you better off…" "Debating Our Destiny"; p.71 "Require…our best effort…" *The Public Papers*; p.74 "It's time to recognize…" *ibid.*; p.75 "People like him as

an individual…" *Role of a Lifetime*, 91; p.75 "You specified that you wanted…" *The Reagan Diaries*, x; p.77 "The car took off. I sat up…" *ibid.*, 12; p.77 "Honey, I forgot to duck…I hope you're…" *President Reagan*, 36; p.77 "We're all Republicans today," *ibid.*, 38; p.78 "Whatever happens now…" *The Reagan Diaries*, 12; p.79 "Commit any crime…" *The Public Papers*, p.80 "None of us understands…" *President Reagan*, 96; p.81 "A growing suspicion that the president…" *ibid.*, 120; p.82 "Ash heap of history," *The Public Papers*; p.84 "Many Americans are wondering…" *ibid.*; p.86 "Could intercept and destroy…" *ibid.*; p.87 "Even if a nuclear war…" *An American Life*, 550; p.88 "This is an act violating…" *Ronald Reagan*, 151; p.90 "It's morning again in America…" "Reagan," *American Experience*; p.91 "I saw the election as approval…" *An American Life*, 331; p.92 "I want you to do whatever…" *Ronald Reagan*, 157; p.94 "President Reagan told me…" *For the Soul of Mankind*, 365; p.94 "I would hope that this common ground…" *An American Life*, 630–631; p.95 "Second American Revolution," *President Reagan*, 256; p.95 "There was something likeable…" *An American Life*, 635; p.96 "Trust, but verify," *ibid.*, 699; p.97 "A fresh start in relations…" *President Reagan*, 294; p.99 "It is a complex undertaking…" *The Reagan Diaries*, 374; p.99 "We're not dealing with terrorists." *President Reagan*, 298; p.101 "There is no government connection…" *ibid.*, 338; p.101 "I authorized the transfer of small amounts…" *The Public Papers*; p.103 "As a confused and remote figure…" "The White House Crisis"; p.104 "Now what should happen…" *The Public Papers*; p.105 "The fact of the matter is…" *ibid.*; p.105 "Created the condition which made possible…" *Final Report*, Chapter 27; p.109 "General Secretary Gorbachev…" *The Public Papers*; p.110 "For the first time in history…" *ibid.*; p.112 "Go out there and win…" *President Reagan*, 477; p.113 "Some things haven't changed," *An American Life*, 709; p.113 "I was talking about another time…" *President Reagan*, 473; p.115 "Two triumphs, two things…" *The Public Papers*; p.115 "Tomorrow I stop being president," *The Reagan Diaries*, 692; p.118 "We stood tall and proclaimed…" "Address at Republican National Convention"; p.119 "It might promote greater awareness…" *Reagan, In His Own Hand*, 499.

125

Bibliography

"Arms, Hostages and Contras: How a Secret Foreign Policy Unraveled." *New York Times*, November 19, 1987.

Biven, W. Carl. *Jimmy Carter's Economy*. Chapel Hill: University of North Carolina Press, 2002.

Burbank, Garin. "Governor Reagan and California Welfare Reform: The Grand Compromise of 1971." *California History*, Vol. 70, No. 3 (Fall, 1991), pp. 278–289.

_____. "Governor Reagan's Only Defeat: The Proposition 1 Campaign in 1973." *California History*, Vol. 72, No.43 (Winter, 1993/1994), pp. 360–373.

Calvin Coolidge Memorial Foundation, http://www. calvin-coolidge.org/html/the_business_of_america_ is_bus.html.

Cannon, Lou. *President Reagan: The Role of a Lifetime.* New York: Public Affairs, 2000.

Cannon, Lou, and Carl M. Cannon. *Reagan's Disciple: George W. Bush's Troubled Quest for a Presidential Legacy*. New York: Public Affairs, 2008.

Ceplair, Larry, and Steven Englund. *The Inquisition in Hollywood: Politics in the Film Community, 1930–1960*. Berkeley: University of California Press, 1983.

Conason, Joe. "Reagan Without Sentimentality." Salon.com, June 8, 2004, http://dir.salon.com/story/ opinion/conason/2004/06/08/reagan/index.html.

"Debating Our Destiny." *PBS NewsHour*, October 28, 1980.

Diggins, John Patrick. *Ronald Reagan: Fate, Freedom, and the Making of History*. New York: W.W. Norton & Company, 2007.

Evans, Rowland, and Robert Novak. "'Noncandidate' Reagan Eyes Convention Conquest." *Milwaukee Sentinel*, September 18, 1967, p. 16.

Final Report of The Independent Counsel for Iran/ Contra Matters. Volume 1. August 4, 1993.

House Un-American Activities Committee Testimony of Ronald Reagan, October 23, 1947.

Isaacs, Jeremy, and Downing, Taylor. *Cold War: An Illustrated History, 1945–1991*. Boston: Little, Brown and Company, 1998.

"Jimmy Carter." *American Experience*, http://www.pbs. org/wgbh/amex/carter/index.html.

Marley, David John. *Pat Robertson: An American Life*. Lanham, MD: Rowan & Littlefield, 2007.

Kengor, Paul. "A Pair for History." *National Review* Online, December 27, 2006, http://article. nationalreview.com/301823/a-pair-for-history/paul-kengor.

Leffler, Melvyn P. *For the Soul of Mankind: The United States, the Soviet Union, and the Cold War*. New York: Hill and Wang, 2007.

Neuman, Johanna. "Former President Reagan Dies at 93." *Los Angeles Times*, June 6, 2004.

Reagan, Ronald. "Address at Republican National Convention," August 17, 1992.

_____. *An American Life*. New York: Simon and Schuster, 1990.

_____. "Official Announcement for President," November 13, 1979.

_____. *The Public Papers of President Ronald W. Reagan*. Ronald Reagan Presidential Library.

_____. *The Reagan Diaries*. Edited by Douglas Brinkley. New York: Harper Perennial, 2007.

"Reagan." *American Experience*, http://www.pbs.org/ wgbh/amex/reagan/index.html.

Reeves, Richard. *President Reagan: The Triumph of Imagination*. New York: Simon and Schuster Paperbacks, 2005.

Roberts, Steven V. "The White House Crisis." *New York Times*, February 27, 1987.

Screen Actors Guild History, http://www.sag.org/ history.

Skinner, Kiron K., Annelise Anderson, and Martin Anderson, eds. *Reagan, In His Own Hand*. New York: Touchstone, 2002.

Tygiel, Jules. *Ronald Reagan and the Triumph of American Conservatism*. New York: Pearson Longman, 2005.

Weisman, Steven R. "Reagan Blames 'Great Society' for Economic Woes." *New York Times*, May 10, 1983.

Wills, Garry. *Reagan's America: Innocents at Home*. Garden City, NY: Doubleday and Company, 1987.

Wines, Michael. "President Offers Apology." *Eugene Register-Guard*, August 13, 1987, p. 1A.

Wittner, Lawrence S. "Reagan and Nuclear Disarmament." *Boston Review*, http://bostonreview. net/BR25.2/wittner.html.

Index

Afghanistan 68, 79, 91, *91*, 108–109
Berlin Wall *108–109*, 109, *116*, 116–117
Bush, Pres. George
  pres. campaigns *66*, 67, 68, 112, 113, *113*
  as pres. 105, 115
  at Reagan Pres. Library 117
  as vice pres. *72*, 105, 112
Bush, Pres. George W. *120*
California
  economics 51–52, 57–58
  Hollywood 22–23, *23*, *33*, 33–34
  home in Bel Air 115, 120
  political trip 47–48, *47–48*
  Pres. Library 117, *117*
  ranch *41*, 115, 119, *119*
  Watts riots 49
Carter, Pres. Jimmy *62*, 62–66, *68*, 69–70, 73, 117
Cold War
  and Afghanistan 108–109
  and Cuba 43, *43*
  end 117–118
  and Germany. *See* Berlin Wall
  and Latin America 88. *See also* contras
  and the Soviet Union 30, 86, 92–93. *See also* Gorbachev, Mikhail; nuclear weapons
  and the Vietnam War 49
Communism
  in Afghanistan 68, 79
  in Grenada 84–85
  in Latin America 79–80, 82, 88
  in the Soviet Union 7, 7, 30–31, 79, 81, 93, 95, 117–118
  in the U.S. 30–34
conservatives 37, 66–67, 78, 89, 92, 111–112, 120
Constitution 89, *89*, 106, 107
contras 79–80
contras, U.S. aid to
  Congr. opposition 82, 94
  illegal 82, *88*, 88–89, 91–92, 100
  Iran-contra affair *98*, 99–105, *100–104*
Cuba 43, 85
Democratic Party 47, 51, 59, 106
Disciples of Christ 12, 13, 14
economics
  Calif. crisis 51–52, 57–58
  Depression 16–17, *17*, 18–19, 27, 30
  inflation 64, 68, 73–74, 107
  recession 80
  savings and loan crisis 107
  supply-side 74
  tax reform *94*, 94–95

Ford, Pres. Gerald 58, 60, 61, *61*, 62, 63, 68, 117
Germany 27, 29, 30. *See also* Berlin Wall
Goldwater, Sen. Barry 44–45, *44–45*, 46, 88
Gorbachev, Mikhail
  background 93, *93*
  at end of the Cold War 117–118
  INF treaty 110, *110*, 111
  summit mtgs. 6, 6–9, *9*, 95–97, *95–97*, 112–113, 114
  visit to Reagan's ranch 119, *119*
The Great Society 56
Grenada 84–85, *85*
Illinois 10, *10*, 12, 14, 39
Iran
  hostage crisis of 1979 64–65, *65*, 68–69, 70–71
  Iran-contra affair *98*, 99–105, *100–104*
  Iran-Iraq War 92, 99, *99*
  revolution 64
Iraq 92, 99, *99*
Israel 83, 92, 99
Japan 27, 28, 29, 30
Johnson, Pres. Lyndon B. 13, 56, *56*
Kennedy, Pres. John F. 42, 43, *43*
Khomeini, Ayatollah 65, 99–100
Latin America 79–80
Lebanon 82–84, *82–84*, 85, 98, 99–100
liberals 37, 44–45, 66, 75, 120
McCarthyism 32, *32*
New Deal 19, 27, 32, 56
Nicaragua 79, *79*, 80, 82, 100, *100*. *See also* contras
Nixon, Pres. Richard
  détente 63
  mtg. with Reagan *55*
  pres. campaigns 37, 41, 42, *53*, 62
  at Reagan Pres. Library 117
  Watergate 58, *58*, 59, 62
North, Oliver 100, 102, 104, *104*
nuclear weapons
  arms control 7–9, 63, 93–94, 96–97, 108, 110, 111, 112
  arms race *40*, 40–41, 43, 45, 63, 95
  defense 92. *See also* Strategic Defense Initiative
  INF 108, 110, *110*, 111
  U.S. bombing of Japan 29, *29*
oil industry 64
O'Neill, Tip 75, *75*, 91
prayer 89, *89*
pres. election process 52, *52*
racial issues 31, 49
Reagan, Jack (father) 10–13, *11*, 19, 26, 56
Reagan, Maureen (daughter) *24*, 25
Reagan, Michael (son) 34

Reagan, Nancy (wife)
  belief in astrology 74
  at the ranch *41*, *119*
  support during husband's last years 119
  support of husband's career *50*, *53*, *57*, *67*, 73, *102*, *113*, *114*
  wedding *34*, 35
Reagan, Neil (brother) *11*, 12, 19, 32–33
Reagan, Nelle (mother) 10, *11*, 11–12, 13, 26
Reagan, Patti (daughter) 35
Reagan, Pres. Ronald Wilson "Dutch"
  autobiographies 35, *46*, 46–47, 116
  education 13, 14–16
  entertainment career
    foundation 13, 14
    radio 18, *18*, 20–21, 20–22, 59, 63, *63*
    film 22–26, *25–26*, 28, *35*, 35–36, 42
    SAG president 32, *33*, 34
    television 36, 42
  factual errors in speeches 48, 101
  health
    after the shooting *78*
    Alzheimer's disease 119, 120
    eyesight 14, 22, 28
    hearing 111
    memory 111, 119
    surgery 103
  life
    early years *10*, *11*; 11–14
    college years 14–17, *15–16*
    young adulthood 17–18, 20–26
    first marriage *24*, 25, 34–35
    military service *28*, 28–29
    second marriage *34*, 35
    assassination attempt 76–77, *76–77*
    last years 114–120
    death 120, *120*
    legacy 117–118, 121
  love of horses 21, 24, 41, *41*, 115, *121*
  newspaper column 59, 63
  personality 8, 12, 24, 48, 121
  political career
    foundation 37, 38–40, *39*, 42, *42*
    pres. campaign of 1964 *44*, 44–45, 46
    gov. campaign of 1966 47–50
    as gov. of Calif. *50–51*, 50–52, 54–58
    pres. campaign of 1968 52–53, *53*

pres. campaign of 1976
  57–61, 60, 61
pres. campaign of 1980 9,
  65–71, 66–71
as pres., 1981–1985 72–73,
  72–85
pres. campaign of 1984 9,
  87, 89–91
as pres., 1985–1989 86–97,
  98–105, 106–113,
  114–115
summit mtgs. See under
  Gorbachev, Mikhail
Iran-contra affair 99–105,
  101–103
religious beliefs 12, 13, 77–78
Reagan, Ron (son) 41
Republican Party 32, 37, 42, 43, 45,
  47, 53, 60

Ronald Reagan Presidential Library
  117, 117
Roosevelt, Pres. Franklin D. 19,
  19, 27, 32
Sandinistas 79. See also contras
Screen Actors Guild (SAG) 31,
  31–34, 33
Shultz, George 92, 94, 101, 108
Soviet Union. See also allied
  countries; Cold War
  and the Berlin Wall 109, 109,
  117
  break-up 117, 120
  Reagan's visit to 112, 112–113
  under Stalin 30, 31
  war in Afghanistan 68, 79, 91,
  91, 108–109
Strategic Defense Initiative (SDI)
  7–9, 86–87, 86–87, 96, 97, 118

Supreme Court 106–107, 107
terrorism 82, 82–84, 84, 99–100.
  See also Iran, hostage crisis
  of 1979
United States. See also Cold War;
  Vietnam War
  INF treaty 110, 110, 111
  Iran and foreign policy 64–65
  and Nicaragua. See contras
  Vietnam War 48, 49, 49, 54
  and war in Afghanistan 79, 91,
  91, 108–109
  WWII 27–29, 29, 30
Vietnam War 48, 49, 49, 54
welfare reform 55–57
World War II 27–28, 27–30
Wyman, Jane (wife) 24, 24–25,
  34–35

Acknowledgments

The author would like to thank Tom Paterson for his many expert insights on the Cold War over the years, Jim Buckley for his ongoing support, Lou Cannon for his expertise, and John Searcy at DK Publishing for his skill and patience.

Picture Credits

Photo Research by *Anne Burns Images*

Front Cover Photo by *Ronald Reagan Presidential Library*

Back Cover Photo by *Corbis/David & Janice Frent Collection*

The photographs in this book are used with permission and through the courtesy of:

Getty Images: pp.1, 19, 38, 66, 94, 98, 116, 122tl; NY Daily News; p.70 Time & Life Pictures. *Ronald Reagan Presidential Library:* pp.2–3, 4–5, 6, 9, 11, 12, 15, 16, 21, 25, 26, 28, 34, 36, 39, 42, 44, 50, 55, 56, 57, 58, 67, 71, 72, 73, 75, 76, 77, 78, 80, 85, 86, 90, 95, 96, 101, 103, 106, 108, 110, 112, 114, 115, 117, 121, 122tc, 122br, 123tl & tc, 123 bl & br. Corbis:* p.7 Elio Ciol; pp.17, 18, 22, 24, 29, 30, 31, 33, 41, 43, 45, 48, 49, 53, 60, 63, 69, 83, 89, 107, 113, 122tr Bettman; p.23 John Springer Collection; p.27 Hulton Deutsch Collection; pp.35, 87, 122bl, 123tc David & Janice Frent Collection; pp.40, 92 Roger Ressmeyer; p.47 Travel Pix; pp.51, 54 Ted Streshinsky; p.52 Wally McNamee; p.62 George Tiedemann; p.64 R. Krubner; p.65 Kevin Kazemi; p.79 John Giannini; p.81 White House; pp.82, 99 Francoise Demulder; p.84 Jean Guichard; p.88 Bill Gentile; p.91 Reza Webiston; pp.93, 109 Peter Turnley; p.100 Andrew Holbrooke; p.118 Rolf-Finn Hestoff; p.119 Reuters; p.120 William Philpott. *Unknown Photographer, 56th Field Artillery Command, U.S. Army/Europe:* p.8. John Delano, Hammond, Indiana:* pp.10, 122tl. Ronald Reagan Boyhood Home:* p.14. National Baseball Hall of Fame Library:* p.20. Library of Congress:* p.32. Smithsonian Institution:* p.37. DK Publishing:* p.46 Jessica Park. Executive Office of the President:* p.61. Jimmy Carter Presidential Library:* p.68. Alamy Images:* p.74 Tetra Images. Laurentgauthier:* p.97. Associated Press:* pp.102, 104. Ukranian Air Force Museum:* p.111.

Border Images, left to right: *Ronald Reagan Presidential Library, Library of Congress, Ronald Reagan Presidential Library, Ronald Reagan Presidential Library, Ronald Reagan Presidential Library, Ronald Reagan Presidential Library.*

Other DK Biographies you'll enjoy:

Abigail Adams
Kem Knapp Sawyer
ISBN 978-0-7566-5209-8 paperback
ISBN 978-0-7566-5208-1 hardcover

Marie Curie
Vicki Cobb
ISBN 978-0-7566-3831-3 paperback
ISBN 978-0-7566-3832-0 hardcover

Charles Darwin
David C. King
ISBN 978-0-7566-2554-2 paperback
ISBN 978-0-7566-2555-9 hardcover

Princess Diana
Joanne Mattern
ISBN 978-0-7566-1614-4 paperback
ISBN 978-0-7566-1613-7 hardcover

Amelia Earhart
Tanya Lee Stone
ISBN 978-0-7566-2552-8 paperback
ISBN 978-0-7566-2553-5 hardcover

Thomas Edison
Jan Adkins
ISBN 978-0-7566-5207-4 paperback
ISBN 978-0-7566-5206-7 hardcover

Albert Einstein
Frieda Wishinsky
ISBN 978-0-7566-1247-4 paperback
ISBN 978-0-7566-1248-1 hardcover

Benjamin Franklin
Stephen Krensky
ISBN 978-0-7566-3528-2 paperback
ISBN 978-0-7566-3529-9 hardcover

Gandhi
Amy Pastan
ISBN 978-0-7566-2111-7 paperback
ISBN 978-0-7566-2112-4 hardcover

Harry Houdini
Vicki Cobb
ISBN 978-0-7566-1245-0 paperback
ISBN 978-0-7566-1246-7 hardcover

Thomas Jefferson
Jacqueline Ching
ISBN 978-0-7566-4506-9 paperback
ISBN 978-0-7566-4505-2 hardcover

Helen Keller
Leslie Garrett
ISBN 978-0-7566-0339-7 paperback
ISBN 978-0-7566-0488-2 hardcover

Joan of Arc
Kathleen Kudlinksi
ISBN 978-0-7566-3526-8 paperback
ISBN 978-0-7566-3527-5 hardcover

John F. Kennedy
Howard S. Kaplan
ISBN 978-0-7566-0340-3 paperback
ISBN 978-0-7566-0489-9 hardcover

Martin Luther King, Jr.
Amy Pastan
ISBN 978-0-7566-0342-7 paperback
ISBN 978-0-7566-0491-2 hardcover

Abraham Lincoln
Tanya Lee Stone
ISBN 978-0-7566-0834-7 paperback
ISBN 978-0-7566-0833-0 hardcover

Nelson Mandela
Lenny Hort & Laaren Brown
ISBN 978-0-7566-2109-4 paperback
ISBN 978-0-7566-2110-0 hardcover

Mother Teresa
Maya Gold
ISBN 978-0-7566-3880-1 paperback
ISBN 978-0-7566-3881-8 hardcover

Annie Oakley
Chuck Wills
ISBN 978-0-7566-2997-7 paperback
ISBN 978-0-7566-2986-1 hardcover

Barack Obama
Stephen Krensky
ISBN 978-0-7566-5805-2 paperback
ISBN 978-0-7566-5804-5 hardcover

Pelé
Jim Buckley
ISBN 978-0-7566-2987-8 paperback
ISBN 978-0-7566-2996-0 hardcover

Eleanor Roosevelt
Kem Knapp Sawyer
ISBN 978-0-7566-1496-6 paperback
ISBN 978-0-7566-1495-9 hardcover

Harriet Tubman
Kem Knapp Sawyer
ISBN 978-0-7566-5806-9 paperback
ISBN 978-0-7566-5807-6 hardcover

George Washington
Lenny Hort
ISBN 978-0-7566-0835-4 paperback
ISBN 978-0-7566-0832-3 hardcover

Laura Ingalls Wilder
Tanya Lee Stone
ISBN 978-0-7566-4508-3 paperback
ISBN 978-0-7566-4507-6 hardcover